Girls Do IT Too

Sonja Bernhardt OAM

Every effort has been made to trace or contact all copyright holders. The author and publisher will be pleased to make good any omissions or rectify any mistakes bought to their attention at the earliest opportunity.

The names and identifying details of some of the people mentioned in this book have been changed.

Sonja Bernhardt OAM has a moral right to be identified as the author of this work. The memories related are her memories. If anything is in error it is in error in her memories.

Copyright © 2020 Sonja Bernhardt OAM

Published by ThoughtWare Books

All rights reserved.

ISBN: 978-0-6484972-7-1

DEDICATION

To everything WIT in my life: All the women in technology in the world, the WiT (Qld) organisation and of course to my witty husband☺

CONTENTS

THE START 1

    1 My Birth and Childhood 3

    2 20/20 Hindsight 15

    3 Climbing the Lattice 27

THE SOCIALISING 47

    4 WIT's Birth and Almost a Funeral 49

    5 Networking Madness 57

    6 The Award and Credibility Tango 77

    7 Sonja in Wonderland 89

THE BUSINESS BUILD AND GROWTH 117

    8 The Business Birth and Pivots 119

    9 The Size is Right 127

    10 Growing Pains 139

    11 Follow the Money 153

    12 To Be or Not to Be 167

THE SALE AND END OF AN ERA 195

    13 The Twilight Zone 197

    14 To Retirement and Beyond 209

Epilogue 217

About the Author 223

Notes 224

ACKNOWLEDGMENTS

To my parents for your great DNA and living your life of integrity and being strong role models.

To Robin and Lorraine for your reviews, comments, edits and on-going encouragement.

To Edwina Shaw for adding the polish to make this memoir zing.

To Lynelle for sourcing the Lattice photos, no idea why I didn't have any when it was such a formative time of my life.

To El Blaney from Foundry Productions for the authentic cover photo of me taken before I even decided to write my memoirs, but it is so perfect.

To Renee Sanson (my daughter in law) for the stunning back picture, taken when we were on our family cruise Christmas/New Year 2020. Also thanks for doing such a wonderful job with Noah, Ava and Ella, my three fabulous grandchildren all of whom probably know more about technology than I do.

PREFACE

Whilst I have lived my life as a mixture of personal and business to ensure the whole of me is engaged into all my activities I did, when it came to writing my memoirs it made sense to divide the book into two distinct parts. The first seven chapters are personal storytelling and written as such. The remaining seven chapters adopt a more formal business tone. I hope that as the reader you find both sections of interest and enjoy my tale and all the life lessons that come with it.

The Start

Girls Do IT Too

1 My Birth and Childhood

Making an Entrance

> *A woman's life can really be a succession of lives, each revolving around some emotionally compelling situation or challenge, and each marked off by some intense experience – Wallis Simpson, Duchess of Windsor*

Yahoo!

Multi-millionaire!

I am a multi-millionaire! Woohoo!

There, I've said it, even shouted it. I have achieved my dream goal and the dream for many entrepreneurs. As one of those supposedly "rare" females in technology, I have successfully exited my software development business. Not only successfully, but for returns that made it all worthwhile.

It wasn't just the money that made it valuable after years of mammoth effort and all-consuming work. Why else would entrepreneurs do it if we didn't enjoy or value the journey? Making it financially worthwhile is only the practical reward for all those years, fears and tears – the physical manifestation of creating, nurturing, living and breathing the business every second of every day.

The legal contract was signed and sealed, the sale price was as agreed and the money was mine, but I wouldn't get it all in one payment. It would be paid into my bank account over a few years.

I approached this extended payment plan with some scepticism, given that my life in business had taught me that "a deal is not a deal until the money is in the bank". A difficult lesson to learn, and one I learnt the hard way through experiencing the joy of a prospect agreeing to be a client, then having them back out before they banked the funds. With that lesson in mind and with the funds from this company exit sale to follow over time, I felt some trepidation. But hey, it was agreed, signed and legal and I wouldn't be spending all the money up front anyway. Having it come in on a regular basis seemed a good idea and brought some thoughts of future security. When the money hits the bank does not impact the valuation and sale price. Multi-Millionaire I am.

It took six months for me to begin to feel that it was *real*. The agreement to sell happened in February 2020, just before the entire world faced war with the Coronavirus, which raged through every country and impacted upon every area of life, disrupting social, economic and health factors globally. In parallel I was waging my own life-change war, with all the impacts from selling and saying goodbye to software that I had lived and breathed and poured my entire self into for fifteen years. Having given it life, so much of my life, I was naturally experiencing and trying to manage the unexpected effects of "selling my baby".

How did I, a university dropout, single parent, who'd been sacked from a corporate role, and been through a series of health scares, manage to sell my company and become a multi-millionaire? How did I tackle the "bro" world of technology to build a value adding technology platform and come out the other end with more money than I can even work out what to do with in this unknown world? How can you learn from what I've achieved and the mistakes I've made, to potentially do the same yourself… without making the mistakes?

This is my story of what, where, how, when and why this woman got IT.

This is my story of that journey with all the figurative and literal blood, sweat and tears. A journey surrounded by exuberance and triumphs, from birthing and then growing then finally selling my baby: my software development business.

First Birth

I was in a hurry to be born. My dad, mum and her older sister jumped into the one-seater Holden ute and headed off at top speed on the 50 kilometre journey from George Town to Launceston, Tasmania.

Dad was pulled over for speeding at Mowbray (a suburb of Launceston), but after one glance at my mother, the police forgave the speeding and let us continue. That was just in time, as on 26 March 1959, I was born on a stretcher going through the front door of the Queen Victoria Hospital.

My mother always said I was in a rush to get out and start talking. This has rung true throughout my life and career, time and time again.

I was the first-born daughter, the third and middle child of a family of five children. My father, Helmut, emigrated from Germany after World War II, becoming part of the construction crew that helped expand the township of George Town in Tasmania, where I lived for the first ten years of my life.

I grew up with stories of Dad's arrival as a migrant. On his first day at work when he was asked to say his name, he proudly replied in his thick German accent, "Helmut Ernst Siegfried Bernhardt!" I could almost hear his efficient German heels clicking as he said it. The crew supervisor said, "Geez, mate, you won't get far here with a name like that! We'd better call you Tom."

And so Tom he became. It wasn't until his older years that he reverted to his true name and identity.

My dad was a handsome, dashing, exotic foreigner who roared around on a motorbike. He was a master painter and decorator, a table tennis champion, a talented trumpet, piano and drums player, and an amazing dancer whose fast-moving feet were incredible to watch. My mother, Olive (nee James) was a primary school teacher in George Town at that time, and they met and fell in love at a table tennis match. He won the table tennis championship but more importantly he easily won Mum's heart and they married in 1955.

My mother is from a very large family from the Scottsdale region of Tasmania. All jokes aside, or perhaps confirmed, I have relatives galore in almost every town in Tasmania, except my own brothers and sisters and their offspring who now all live on the mainland.

Both of my parents were determined individuals with strong work ethics. Both committed time and energy to various committees and activities. I fondly remember sneaking sandwich cut-offs from catering Mum did as part of her work on the Golf Club committee, in addition to the work she did assisting with committee bookkeeping and meetings.

It is fair to say that I definitely inherited those characteristics and behaviours from my parents. Not the motorbike riding, music playing or table tennis, as I don't have a musical or sports bone anywhere in my body, but the determination, passionate volunteering and a strong work ethic that are my core drivers.

My childhood memories are full of family holidays, hours of being happily lost in my imagination, exploring rock pools at the beach, engaging in hijinks with my siblings – especially laughing a lot with my sisters Susan and Sarah over the pranks my brothers Paul and Peter played. Even when one of those pranks was to pull a table out from under me that I was joyously "skating on" in my socks. I fractured my collarbone. Another prank convinced me I could fly off the garden fence, with more injuries ensuing.

Being knocked down and getting back up to face the "injury" was a lesson that came in handy later when running my own business. But perhaps a key to my final success was failing to learn that I could *not* do the impossible from the flying prank.

On weekends the radio blared from our house with news, news and more news – Dad loved (was almost obsessed with) repeated playing of the radio news every hour and later on TV. He roared with laughter at TV shows like *Hogan's Heroes* and he just loved war movies. Oddly enough Dad never taught us to speak German (I may have learnt a few German swear words though), but we did live in a house with cuckoo clocks, beer steins, roast pork, pickled pork and stinky cheese.

Ahhh… stinky cheese. Dad's Germanic love of meat and cheese. It's amazing how much smell stirs memories. One whiff of that extra pungent cheese instantly takes me back in time. Another "time machine" for me is oranges.

When I was around eight or nine, I was walking to school and eating an orange and, as my mother predicted, talking at the same time. A fly flew into my mouth and buzzed around, and to this day I still remember the feeling of that fly and my own disgust. So much so that in an irrational response even today I still avoid eating oranges and drinking orange juice. This is obviously selective irrationality as it doesn't stop me consuming Cointreau or chocolate-covered orange strips. Apparently, the right additives can overcome almost anything.

Changing Landscapes

In June 1969, when I was ten, my childhood changed. My father may have started in George Town as a master painter, but over time he expanded and by then he owned a few businesses, including an overseas shipping supply office, glass and paint shop and a food outlet at Bell Bay.

We lived in what was considered a comfortable middle-class house, even if the toilet was still outside the house! We had not one, but two driveways, where the pride of our cars, a shiny Mercedes, stood gleaming. I recall house help, not live in, but nanny style. Dad used to have trips overseas, some may have just been to the mainland but to us that was still overseas. He always used to bring us back surprise gifts. My sister Susan and I had the first Barbie™ Dolls in the township. Barbie™ was released in 1959, the year of my birth, but it wasn't until 1964 that they went on sale in Melbourne: so I imagine those dolls we had, if we still had them, would be worth a fair bit of money these days.

I vividly recall a night when there was some noise coming from the kitchen area and I really needed to go to the toilet so left my room and crept out. To get to the outside toilet I had to go through the kitchen where, to my shock, my parents were engaged in a noisy disagreement and Dad had even thrown a kitchen chair or two in frustration, not at Mum but onto the wall or floor where they had broken. Mum and Dad spoke to me gently and waited while I went to the toilet.

At that time my main concern was where was I going to sit to eat breakfast! What I did not know was that unfortunately, despite his incredible work efforts, Dad's multiple business deals and activities had fallen apart and our world was beginning to crumble. He owed a large debt and was declared bankrupt.

Despite the initial frustrations he and Mum had felt, bankruptcy brought out the best in them – characteristics of strength of character, tenacity and that unstoppable work ethic. Instead of falling apart or leaving his family to fend for themselves, in 1969, in a brave and daring move, Dad packed us all up, moved across the state to Zeehan and started life all over again.

To us kids it was an adventure. Despite my one night-time toilet trip insight into the looming issue, we children had no idea of the reason behind the change and everything seemed like an exciting new adventure. The luxurious Mercedes was replaced with a practical Falcon, Dad's overseas trips stopped along with the surprise gifts, and there was no nanny or house assistants, but it was smooth and easy to adjust. Besides, as kids, home was stable and we rapidly got busy seeking out new friends in our new township.

Zeehan was built in the 1800s, funded from an economic boom after tin, silver and lead were discovered there. It was a little like a Wild West town for Tasmania, where rugged Victorian-era miners had once stayed and played. It even earned the nickname of Silver City. By the time we arrived its heyday was long gone, and it was almost a ghost town, but it had some majestic looking buildings. One of the most majestic was the Gaiety Theatre, where Dame Nellie Melba had once performed to a packed house.

Our arrival coincided with a new release of tin mining by Renison Bell nearby, and a subsequent resurgence in the township. I can't say I lived in the Wild West, but I lived in its shadow and certainly got to see a town with the scars left from having gone from boom to bust. Reflecting what I would see later in life watching businesses go from boom to bust to boom to bust. Thoughts of "Sonja get your guns" ring in my head…

Dad began as a shop assistant in Howards Hardware Store, and within a few years built his way back up the ladder to Purchasing Manager for Renison Bell, the mining giant. Mum, being the trouper she was, also secured work, first at the local Moyles Hotel in the restaurant and housekeeping area plus as a teacher, then later at Renison Bell in accounts and administration. Both Mum and Dad also became active township community members, demonstrating major strength of character and determination which are key traits that my siblings and I inherited.

As early as Grade Five my genetically inherited traits from the James side of the family of having a full and large bust started to show. I began wearing bras in Grade Five and started to become conscious of the fact that my body was different to many of the other girls. Naturally I suffered some teasing, from both boys and girls. Teasing that after initially stinging taught me to act as if their unkindness didn't mean anything. I just shrugged and took no notice. The teasing reduced if I did not react to it, if I didn't bite back.

Those bras in Grade Five were already a "B" cup size so I was definitely an early stage developer. From then on my breasts just kept growing and ultimately, it got to the stage where I was embarrassed to wear a swimsuit. It was impossible to buy one that fitted my smaller body and ginormous bust. As a result, it wasn't until my adult years that I learnt to swim beyond a dog paddle.

I completed Grades Five and Six at Zeehan Primary School, where (probably after spotting my enthusiasm and volunteer willingness) the principal taught me how to read the weather and report it to the national weather system. I was charged with taking readings from the various weather equipment and dutifully recording them, surveying the clouds and calling in the results as an early "work role" that I performed rain, hail or shine – literally. I loved that role. I felt so proud as I walked to school, recorded and analysed the results and called them in to the Hobart station.

Later in life, I realised the wisdom of the principal's delegation of this task: especially on poor weather days, of which there were a few in Zeehan. He remained snug and warm inside his home or outside socialising and having fun, while I braved the weather and consistently did the weekend weather report.

I attended Murray High School in Queenstown, which involved an exciting bus ride every day back and forth from Zeehan to Queenstown. That bus trip was particularly challenging during the winter months, when frost was abundant and the school bus stop was iced over. It didn't stop me from trying to play knucklebones though, even when it meant having to take my gloves off to throw and catch the knuckles. Perhaps playing knucklebones was where I first practiced persistence and resilience.

The unforgettable view of the naked mountains as the school bus descended the hill into Queenstown is an image that has never left me. The unusual and eerie landscape was often referred to as a moonscape. The stark, naked appearance was due to the impacts of earlier mining, when the trees were cut down for use and the sulphur fumes from the mining town copper smelter restricted regrowth. It was certainly different to the usual heavily timbered rainforests of the area, and really stood out.

It was at Murray High School that I enthusiastically dived headlong into debating. School teams travelled the state for inter-school sport championships and while I have zero sporting talent, luckily for me debating was considered an inter-school sport so I got to join the travelling teams. I even got to go back to George Town on one trip. I continued debating throughout my school and university days. Today I consider that debating was important in developing my skills for public speaking by helping me feel comfortable presenting in public, as well as always being ready to give quick responses to opponents.

Both of my brothers were handsome and naturally attracted admirers. It took me some time to realise that the sudden run of girls who wanted to be my friend, and come over for weekend sleepovers, had more to do with flirting with my brothers than building a friendship with me. After I realised, I became a little more discerning in offering sleepovers and chose my friends more carefully. In future years I would discover that sometimes my role was "token female": is that better or worse than "token friend"?

I spent many a weekend climbing hills and from time to time climbing Mount Zeehan, which wasn't very high nor a hard climb, but the view from the top was 360 degrees and stunning. I used to sit at the top for ages admiring the view. When not climbing hills, I was merrily lost in the middle of blackberry bushes. I was reminded of my love of nature during Coronavirus isolation, so hill climbing and spending time outdoors are things I am going to return to now in my retirement.

Zeehan gave us back a life and Dad repaid his debts. Being driven, Dad sought more advancement and opportunities. In 1974 this led to a new life experience, when we moved to Port Moresby in Papua New Guinea. Leading up to the move, Mum would take out our encyclopedias and world map and we would all listen as she read about the history of the country. We were fascinated, and maybe a little scared, at the differences that new world presented. Mum would trace on the map the route we would take to get there from Launceston across Bass Straight into Melbourne, where we would change planes, then continuing to head further north onto Brisbane, and then crossing Torres Straight onto the final destination of Port Moresby.

We packed up, flew out the day of a wild storm and stayed overnight in Brisbane, just after the Brisbane floods. The combination of our stormy departure with the stink of river mud from the flood during our overnight stay made me feel a little anxious. It all felt like bad omens. The next day we flew into Port Moresby.

As we walked off the plane, we were engulfed in hot thick air that almost instantly covered us all in sweat, even when all we did was just stand there. This was the tropics. We had never experienced anything like it before, the classic "feel like you can cut it with a knife" heat. It was a shock. Even more so in comparison with the cold stormy departure the day before. Strangers in a strange land.

That initial anxiety soon departed, and we settled into a hotel while our house was being finalised. We kids had a wonderful time discovering the local swimming pool and revelling in the sunshine. Dad sat at The Boroko Hotel in Port Moresby looking down with pride at his laughing, sun-browned children and happy wife as we experienced tropical fruits for the first time. His eyes shone and his smile was stretched the widest I'd ever seen it.

When our house was completed we moved from the hotel to a suburb called Gerehu. The suburb was fairly new, and we lived in Stage One along with other expatriates. Gerehu was close to the newly built government administration offices in Waigani, where both my parents had jobs. In 2020, Gerehu has had a colourful history, and is divided into seven stages, home to approximately 20,000 Port Moresby residents.

In Gerehu I experienced being an English-speaking white person surrounded by people of different colours speaking other languages for the first time. I couldn't understand a word. As a young teenager it scared me, then I became fascinated and started to watch more closely and learn some phrases and words in both Pidgin English and Motu. I discovered I was terrible at languages and greatly admired those who were multilingual, but even knowing a few key words helped. It helped me then, and also later when I lived for a short time in Indonesia.

It was on a trip to the supermarket near Waigani that I experienced my first up close view of a local spitting out chewed betel nut. It looked like red blood dripping out of their mouth, staining the footpaths. It both scared and shocked me. However, like many things, I learned it was easy to recover from the shock when I realised it was part of the culture and experience. I was never brave enough to try betel nut myself though.

I attended Port Moresby High School to complete the remaining half of Year 10. I wasn't there long, but I noticed a very different school style, a combination of the heat and the different curriculum. I tried to explain to my physical education teacher that I was fairly useless at sport, but she insisted I jump over the gymnastics jumping vault anyway, because it was part of the course and "everyone else" was doing it. She almost bullied me into giving it a go, so under pressure I did attempt it. Alas my fear was proven, and I ended up with a trip to the local hospital for a broken arm. Boy did I show that teacher!

For the first time I studied history and fell in love with it. Due to changing from the Tasmanian school system to the New South Wales system (which is what Papua New Guinea followed), I missed out on studying Biology in year 10 but repeated Macbeth in English. Then I did Macbeth again in year 11, when I moved to Saint Anne's boarding school in Townsville and studied under the Queensland curriculum. So, I'm well versed in small Shakespearean phrases such as, "What, you egg?" and "Out, damned spot!" Such is the renowned "language of Shakespeare" most readily absorbed by schoolkids.

As a family, when we kids were not away at boarding school, our Sundays at home were idyllic. We would go to the library at Ela Beach, swap our library books, then wander into the Ela Beach RSL Club for lunch, where Mum and Dad would bump into work colleagues or bridge partners and generally have a relaxing time. I spent lots of that time sitting in the multicoloured wooden chairs enjoying the beach view and absorbing my weekly taste of *Omni* magazine. *Omni* was a science and science fiction magazine, and I was fascinated by what I learnt and the sci-fi stories. It helped fuel my future interest in science and technology. The science fiction of the 60s and 70s is still my favourite.

Apart from the Ela Beach RSL, much socialising (networking!) was done at Club Germania, the Cathay Club and the Yacht Club. Our family spent many a Christmas or New Year at social gatherings at the Cathay Club, as well as celebrating Chinese New Year a month or so later. More than half my friendship group were Chinese, although many, whose parents were expatriates working in PNG, referred to themselves as ABCs, Australian Born Chinese. Being of Germanic heritage and having a strong Germanic sense of timing, there were many occasions where cultural differences played out in time discrepancies and unmet expectations. In the end I just asked people if that was Chinese time (late), German time (early), Melanesian time (anytime), or real time.

Part of my friendship group (or "tribe" as it's often referred to today) was heavily into sailing, especially catamarans. I recall many wonderful sailing weekends. One was more dramatic than wonderful. Two catamarans set out, heading over to one of the islands. As usual on these jaunts, we drank a bit of alcohol on board and when we got there. On the return one of the boats started to capsize. As it tipped, one of the teenage boys grabbed his bottle of bourbon (priorities!) and clutched it tight to his body. He fell onto the boom and suffered severe damage from the broken glass: I heard it was almost castration. A tough lesson to learn about drinking and driving – well, sailing a catamaran!

Dad used to whiz through the streets of Port Moresby in our Suzuki Jeep, with us kids bouncing up and down in the back, as we hit bumps in the road. These drives were full of the spirit of life and the joy of the road as it twisted and turned on our way back home to Gerehu. I especially loved it when we came the back way home, zooming around Paga Hill and passing a pretty village with houses on stilts at Hanuabada then the impressive World War II Ship relic MV Macdhui in the bay. The ship was owned by Burns Philp and had been bombed by the Japanese in 1942, leaving it as a wreck in the harbour. Burns Philp was a significant name in Moresby and was almost everywhere. There were two department stores in town, one BP's (Burns Philp) and the other Steamies (Steamships), and many other warehouses and buildings also bore their name.

Perhaps Port Moresby wasn't as peaceful as I thought. I do recall reports of one school student a few years later, who was unable to attend an exam period because she'd been speared in her leg as she'd ridden pillion on a motorbike going through Hanuabada. She had to be hospitalised. During celebration times rocks were thrown off Paga Hill, and we were always afraid they would hit the car as it travelled along the road below the hillside. Back at boarding school in Townsville, when I told my friends that I got stoned in Papua New Guinea, they smirked and gave me sly looks.

Those School Girl Days

At boarding school either I did something right, or the class I joined had done enough wrong that the school nuns were keen for an alternative, because one usual rule was suspended. Before my arrival, the rule was that any school captain had to have been with the school since Grade 8. That rule was broken when, after only one year, I was appointed Boarding School Captain: perhaps a preliminary kickstart to my future role as CEO?

What was not a starring role for me when I was at boarding school was the school choir. They were desperate for bodies in the choir for church. I can't hold a tune, but I love to sing. Unfortunately, I have a naturally loud voice that is offkey. Well, offkey to everyone except me. I volunteered to be part of the choir, but after a few practice sessions I was "kindly" told that my presence was required to make up the numbers, but could I please just mouth the words and not actually sing! That may have been my first token role in a group as years later, for perceived diversity reasons, I was often the token female on a number of committees. For me, as I learned from the "friends" who were really after my brothers, at first being a "token" stings a little, but then after I picked myself back up, more often than not, I found it amusing not insulting.

At boarding school, we had to undertake "Knicker Checks" – my first introduction to "compliance". Part of our uniform was regulation underwear, and from time to time the nuns would call a spot check where we all had to line up and walk past the head nun's office, pulling up the side of our uniforms to display what underwear we were wearing! If you had non-regulation fancy knickers on, you were punished. The common "trick" was that each class kept a few swimsuits nearby which were the same colour as the regulation knickers, so if caught out people slipped into those. One year the local radio station cottoned on that a knicker check was happening, as the entire school was lined up at the lake. So the radio station announced it live on air, and the main road in front of the school filled up with cars that merrily honked horns as they passed. I can only image the uproar if such a knicker check was conducted today.

Getting to and from boarding school in Australia involved flights. At the airport, I observed that when most of the other boarding school kids got off the plane, they threw themselves into their parents' arms and generous hugging and kissing ensued. My own family was never overly affectionate. No big hugs and kisses for me. Instead, a simple head nod in greeting and chatter on arrival. It didn't mean we were any less delighted to be back together again.

I spent a few trips feeling stressed about the fact we never publicly hugged, so I forced myself to do so on arrival. But it just didn't feel right, so I didn't keep trying. We may not have overtly displayed affection, but the bonds and care were there.

Once, when Dad was away elsewhere in PNG, I saw a blank signed cheque from him in the lounge room. I asked Mum what it was for, and she explained that that was what Dad always did, just in case anything happened so that Mum had full access to the entire bank account. This was pre-internet banking and ATM's, and before women were able to access certain accounts. Years later, at University, my best friend Lorraine Prior (now Milne) taught me how to accept both a compliment and a hug.

Whatever the opinions of the nuns, I thought that the graduating Year 12 Class of 1976 was a bunch of great people, many of whom I am still connected with today.

My experiences in childhood and adolescence formed the fundamental core of who I am. Undergoing and accepting change, seeking happiness wherever I was in whatever circumstances, and seeing and experiencing the strength of character of my parents who were solid role models for me were memories, traits and ideals I leant on in later years.

***

Sonja's Tips: Unexpected circumstances can lead to improved outcomes. Not all "bad news" is bad news!

Girls Do IT Too

2 20/20 Hindsight

Exploring and Enjoying life

Mistakes are part of the dues one pays for a full life —
Sophia Loren

Those were the days my friend, but they did end.

Formative times that contributed to the adult me and my journey in creating, building and selling my software development business, were my university days in the 70s and my first technology corporate role at Mincom in the late 80s and 90s. When living through those times, you don't realise how much even daily activities and friendships imprint on you. And how that imprint shapes your life.

University Days

I had a wild social time at the University of Queensland in Brisbane. I partied and drank too much. I lived in a college on campus and in my second year took on the role of social convenor. What do they say? Those were the days. For me that rings true, my university days in the late 70s opened a whole new world of socialising and networking up to me.

At uni I studied maths because I was good at it, physics because I liked it and computer studies because my career counsellor at school suggested that was what I ought to do. I had no real idea of what I wanted to do with my life, so I just went with the suggestion and was happy to be accepted into a Bachelor of Science degree.

Studying science and maths meant I got to meet a number of students who were studying engineering or medicine as we had cross-over subjects. Those students were the biggest party animals. I wondered how it would be bumping into any of them in later life. One I ran into later was the dentist who saved my life by spotting a life-threatening tumour in my mouth. Another turned up in early 2018 at a Women in Blockchain event where I was the guest speaker. My old party mate, Dr Jane Thomason, is now a globally known and well-respected person in the blockchain and cryptocurrency space, and the lead person who ran the event was thrilled and honoured that Jane had chosen to attend.

During the networking stage, Jane approached me and we had a brief chat. Apparently, I was rather cool to her as I didn't recognise her from uni days. Later Jane jolted my memory: we had been in the same circle of friends at University and had shared many a drink and laugh together four decades earlier. Maybe too many. My brain cells had been wiped out preventing me from recognising her at the event!

My inner circle at university was small. Throughout my life I kept in mind the lesson I learnt from the girls seeking friendship just to get close to my brothers. I tend to put out, "I am woman hear me roar" mixed with, "I am independent leave me alone" vibes.

However, when my brain cells recovered and I cottoned on to who Jane was, we reminisced and ended up being co-authors of two books. One was *Gender Inequity and the Potential for Change in Technology Fields*[i], an updated version of my first book, and the other was *Blockchain Technology for Global Social Change*[ii], which Jane led and kindly involved me in crafting some content and shaping the model. So, you never know who you will bump into when and what will happen next.

Six of us gals from the university college went out on two memorable, impulsive blind dates. In 1978 a US naval ship docked in Brisbane and a local radio station did a call out for girls willing to be blind dates for the Navy Boys, at Thierry Galichet's first Brisbane restaurant, *La Grande Bouffe*. It was indeed interesting, and the food was better than university canteen food, but the night ended poorly. The US Navy guys assumed that the restaurant bill had been taken care of, so they didn't make any payment, and the six of us students had to foot the bill. That was not easy for poor uni students.

However, the experience didn't dampen our enthusiasm. We tried another radio blind date at a later stage. That one was arranged by radio personality Wayne Roberts (known as "Waynee Poo"). My friend Sue Rennick called in and "applied" for us. We won and the date was arranged, but Sue had registered us all with fake names, except for her own. That made for interesting chatter around the table when on occasion one or more of us accidentally called out to the other using her real name. The experience was fun, the restaurant was lovely, and, luckily for us, that time the radio station footed the bill.

In a typical university fun joking occasion I was awarded the college's "Best Pair". I am aware that these days many would consider that offensive and sexual discrimination, however in truth at the time to me it was hilarious, and I along with many others laughed and laughed. Coincidentally(?) at the end of my first year at University I made the decision to have a breast reduction operation because by the time I went to University they were of a significant and difficult size. So large that there were no bras manufactured that I could fit into. Especially none for a large cup but a size 10 or 12 body. These days they do produce such sizes as F and G cup, but back then DD was the largest available. I still have indents in my shoulders from bras trying to hold up their weight.

I underwent the operation in late 1977 and had five pounds cut off each breast. That's five stacks of butter off each, and that's a lot! During the operation and immediately following it a good university friend, Angela Perrers, looked after me and ensured my recovery at her always welcoming family home on the Gold Coast. Years later I engaged Angela in my company for a short stint while she was between jobs.

Before the operation I had mostly hidden myself and my stoop from carrying the weight of my breasts, under over-sized clothing; the rest of my body was regular size but with a ginormous bust and large clothing it was difficult to tell. After the operation, I was delighted to find I could wear shoestring straps and sleeveless outfits. So, I did.

I returned to University in 1978 looking tanned and trim, carrying myself with more self-assurance. In an insight into typical male brains, despite the theory that men generally like large boobs I found that the young men who were my friends during our first year at uni, suddenly started to try to hit on me, the "new me". But it wasn't a new me, I was the same. All that had changed was my physical appearance and clothing choices. The changed approach from those friends shook me. Especially one boy who I'd had a small crush on the previous year but who had steadfastly ignored me, until he saw the physical change. It felt so shallow. I ended up changing friends and charging on through my life with that tough insight.

It was that insight that taught me that some people only care about the surface of a person, yet I knew that to me it was the deeper soul, spirit and mind of a person that attracted me.

Insights aside my university days of partying had their toll and I was not doing well academically. I was loving the life and the genuine friendships, but without passing that only meant one thing. I became a university drop out.

After Dropping Out of Uni

After dropping out of university I was a bit like a wandering hobo, not sure what to do or where to go, with no real focus or life goal. I tried my hand at numerous different work roles, and despite being a wanderer, I learnt life lessons in every role I undertook during that time. I even had children, got married and divorced in that order. Funny the things you do when you are wandering lost.

Three job roles in this in between time period in particular spring to mind. At one time I travelled into rural and remote communities in Queensland selling wine. I quickly discovered that one of the most effective selling methods was to hang out at the local pub, play darts, drink and get to know the locals. Once we were all friendly, selling the wine was easy. To this day I am still a lousy darts player, though I do improve after a few drinks. The lesson I learnt there was to be genuine. To be myself.

After the success of those sales roles, it's funny that in my own business I found closing software sales such a challenge and always sought out a closer. I was great at building the interest and excitement but, with larger investments, not so good at transferring that excitement into a closed deal. Maybe I fell for the classic error of sales, thinking that a rejection would be personal, and not wanting to face that.

Another job that I tried twice was being a cleaner. I was a complete failure and totally unsuited for that role. I became a housemaid in Brisbane for a while, at a motel near the Story Bridge, but I never liked being a housemaid and wasn't any good at it. That motel is still there, and from time to time as I drive past, I remember my housemaid days.

Another time, in a remote mining community in the central highlands of Queensland, I undertook a job cleaning houses after they had been built in readiness for occupation. The day I accidentally spilled a bucket of water onto brand new carpet ended that job fairly swiftly. My cleaner experience taught me that all roles require skill and that often it is best to let the experts with the right talents do what they do best.

In 1980 when I was living in Western Australia, I became a door-to-door carpet cleaner salesperson. I enjoyed getting out and about and turned out to be not too bad at the job either. The pinnacle of my carpet cleaner sales career was when I sold two carpet cleaners to an elderly fellow who had no carpets! He called into my work office to let them know that he had so thoroughly enjoyed talking to me he was delighted to buy anyway. That sale became the office's leading story. The lesson I learnt from going door to door, was to treat everyone I encounter as interesting people who like to share information and be treated kindly.

My year in Perth, Western Australia, came about from an impulsive decision that was put into action rapidly. At that time, I was working at a popular Brisbane nightclub called The Underground as the "Yummy Tummy girl". My best friend Lorraine had previously held the role, then when she moved on to the Crest Hotel, she recommended me to replace her, which I did. Yummy Tummy was the food station, so I took orders and, if microwaveable or cold I prepared the meals, but if they required chef preparation, I passed them through to the kitchen then called out the name/number when they were ready.

At that time Lorraine was experiencing boyfriend issues and wanted to discuss it after work. We went to what I believe was Brisbane's first all night nightclub located somewhere downstairs off Queen Street. After a long night's work and having a few drinks, we found ourselves still sitting there at five on Saturday morning, making the decision that perhaps the best way to get away from a no-good boyfriend was to… well, get away. Physically pack up and leave. It was an exciting prospect for both of us, so we considered where we'd like to go. We narrowed the list down to Darwin or Perth. As Perth was the furthest away from Brisbane, we agreed that Perth it was, and locked it in.

We both resigned from work that day, collected our final pays, flew out of Brisbane that Sunday and arrived in Perth early Monday morning. We leased an apartment and within a few days I secured a job. A short while later Lorraine also found work. Lorraine and I had an absolute blast in Perth. We spent most of our time partying. We went "clubbing" at least two or three times a week and I still have a fondness for Perth's early 80s club scene: Pinocchio's, Hannibal's, and others, plus the fabulous atmosphere and bands at the Ocean Beach Hotel at Cottesloe.

Despite my experience as the Brisbane Underground's Yummy Tummy girl, I was fairly useless at hospitality work. I tried being a bar waitress at a night club and also a food waitress, once at the airport and another time at a popular pub in Brisbane's Southbank. I was actually sacked from the pub waitress job. My biggest issue, as I saw it, was that I moved fast and was mostly unaware of other bodies near me, so caused many knocks and bumps, or would get in the way of others and clog up passageways. So like cleaning, the lesson I learnt from my hospitality roles was to know what you are good at and what you are not good at, and to let others do the bits you are not good at.

Once I was interviewed for a sales role (not the wine one but another product) that travelled into remote areas of Queensland. I ended that "role" when on the night I arrived at the first township, the business owner I was travelling with booked only one motel room with one bed and then made it clear what he expected. I left immediately and made my own way back to Brisbane, never to speak to him again.

That rattled me a bit, mostly because I'd fallen into such a trap, thinking it was a genuine job. At least I was strong enough to immediately call it for what it was and walk away.

Even before that unexpected sex with the boss role, in one interview I attended the first request the interviewer made was to ask me to parade around in the T-shirt they provided without a bra on. As far as I knew, the job was as a salesperson. Guess what I did? After initially feeling somewhat stunned and confused… Exit left.

I guess what I took from this long list of varied roles is that at least I kept trying; I stretched myself into different roles to ensure I was active, earning and learning.

A Touch of Drama

To my parents it must have seemed that I was living an unsettling and tumultuous life with my ever-changing work jobs. It turned out that work wasn't the only drama in my life during this time.

Dramatic events led to me having my first born "out of wedlock".

The father of my first child saved my life.

I was living in a share house in Brisbane at the time, as was he (Wally). One terrifying night, a criminal broke in, and with a meat cleaver in hand snuck up to the room I was in, seemingly intent on killing. I still remember the chill I felt when, in the very early hours of the morning, the door opened unexpectedly. Wally jumped to my rescue, grabbed his rifle and shot the criminal, who died.

I became a nervous wreck. Wally of course faced court but was found innocent due to self-defense. It was a time of traumatic drama, that in many ways my mind has tried to close off.

What do you do when someone heroically saves your life? Well, I fell into hero-worship for Wally and began an affair with him. With terrible timing, that affair ended when I was fairly heavily pregnant. We were at the Spring Hill Fair in Brisbane, promoted as the first open air street market in Brisbane, created in the style of London's Portobello Road market, where I bumped into some friends from my Papua New Guinea days. I introduced Wally to them, then overheard him telling them that he was leaving Brisbane.

When I asked him about it, he said he was leaving the following week. He had told me nothing about his plans, never even hinted. We were of course together due to the circumstances of the murder attempt and no other reason, but still we'd made a child together. The pregnancy was unexpected, and I knew that marriage had never been on the cards with Wally, but still his abrupt departure, and my secondhand way of hearing about it, was a bit of a shock to me. But what could I do?

Thus at 22 years of age I launched into single parenting. One day a few months later as I was preparing food for a dinner party in the share house I lived in, my waters broke. I was the only person in the house at the time, so I called a taxi and grabbed my "baby ready" bag. I apologized to the taxi driver about the waters mess – he was very kind and soothing and dropped me right at the door of Brisbane Women's Hospital.

At first the nurses did not think I was anywhere near labor, as I was not demonstrating any pain or major stress. So I was placed in a ward, and when I called out after a few minutes saying something was happening, they made some grumbling comments, until with a shock the nurse said, "She's ten centimeters dilated! This baby is coming!"

The room suddenly filled with people and my baby rushed on out. On 8 January 1982, my first daughter Naomi was born. All that happening in less than two hours from water breaking to birth, without any noticeable or remarkable pain. I heard the dinner party went well. I called in from the hospital landline (pre mobile phone days then), to let them know where I had got up to with the food preparation and gave my excuse for not attending. What an excuse it was.

My first born actually didn't have a name at first. With all the events surrounding her birth I simply had not decided upon one, so she remained "No Namie" up until the time came to register her birth. "No Namie" morphed into "Naomi", who was a friend of mine from University days; and for her second name I decided on Lorraine, after my still best buddy, also from my University days.

When Naomi was a baby, she was diagnosed with Hemiplegia Cerebral Palsy (CP) on her right side. In a guilty-mother moment, I wondered if she had been injured during the super-fast birth, if my muscular contractions had pushed into her brain and caused the condition. But that's mothers for you. We tend to worry about lots of things, often irrationally. Fortunately, Naomi's CP was mild. She was able to walk, so wasn't confined to a wheelchair When she was young, we both spent a fair bit of time doing physiotherapy exercises. Those exercises helped her arm and leg muscles. She also needed a small amount of occupational and speech therapy as she grew older and she wore a caliper on her right leg for a few years.

By the time Naomi was five, it was obvious she was as bright as a button but constrained by the caliper. Both she and I agreed the caliper could go. It was more of a clumsy hinderance than a help, so we threw it into a shopping center rubbish bin in Darwin. We walked away together smiling and never looked back, a little like Forrest Gump running into the future.

When Naomi was 12, before she was fully grown, she underwent an operation to cut the size of her good leg down to the length her right one was expected to grow to, so that she wouldn't have unevenness in her leg lengths nor the associated limp.

Then something happened that I felt guilty about for many years. I was trying to get into our gated apartment complex with Naomi and Thomas in the car, but the security gate was stuck and wouldn't open. There was a manual way to open it, but it was only accessible through the pedestrian walk-through gate. As I backed the car away from the security card swipe area to move closer to the pedestrian gate, focusing entirely on reversing, unknown to me Naomi suddenly opened her car door and put her right leg out. I ran over her foot. All three of us erupted into screams and tears.

Back to the hospital. Her right foot was fractured. Naomi had only recently had her good leg operated on, so after the accident had both legs in plaster and was confined to a wheelchair, which was no fun for either of us. Nor for Thomas as the accident had happened on his tenth birthday.

The school Naomi attended didn't have wheelchair access and each day I had to carry her up the stairs to get to her classroom then carry her wheelchair up as well, and repeat the procedure at the end of her school day. That put an immense physical strain on me, on top of my extreme mother guilt. The one good thing about it was that was a wake-up call for the school to make some changes. They ended up installing disabled accessible ramps, but by then Naomi was recovered from the leg casts and didn't require them. At least it was there for other people when it was needed.

The leg shortening operation seemed to work well and today she is still as bright as a button and the only sign of any cerebral palsy tends to only be visible when she is very tired and her right hand curls up.

Years later when she was an independent adult, I surprised Naomi by presenting her with a *Where's Wally* personalised book. I had hired a private detective to track down her biological father then created the book for her including his contact details. She then reached out and made contact with him. Soon afterwards they met, and not much later she travelled to Italy with her paternal grandfather to meet her other relatives.

In 1983, when Naomi was just starting to toddle around, I met my first husband Clive. We were engaged within one month of meeting and married within three months. It is said that fools rush in, and I certainly rushed headfirst into that marriage: Not something I would recommend!

Our son, Thomas Nathan, was born in a rush on 19 May 1984 and it is that birth that led me to think for years that women who complained about childbirth were wussy. Like Naomi he was arriving fast. So fast the doctors tried to slow his birth down by giving me an epidural. He was born before it kicked in, then I stupidly climbed off the bed after the birth, rushing to do something, and fell down as the epidural was then in effect and my legs just didn't want to stand. I was injured in that fall.

The nurses were cross with me and themselves. Apart from the pain of the fall, I experienced little pain and only short-term pain with Thomas's birth. For years, I was secretly thinking that complainers about childbirth were just that, they had low pain thresholds and were exaggerating. I learnt differently during the birth of my third child, more on that later.

It was a turbulent marriage with Clive and a trigger for a major life's change.

The Divorce Pivot

As a family Naomi, Thomas, Clive and I moved around a fair bit, even once living for a short stint near the Whitsunday Islands. Eventually we ended up on Groote Eylandt, in the Gulf of Carpentaria in the Northern Territory.

Clive was the chef at the mining town in the township of Alyangula. Life on Groote was fascinating, a small community with basic living conditions. At that time, it was not the resort-style place it is promoted as today.

The fishing even off the wharf was outstanding, and while I'm not normally into fishing, I was into it there as it was incredible to be able to simply drop a line and pull in a coral trout. While I lived there, every two weeks the township lit up with excitement as fresh flowers were flown in. There were no dress shops until someone set one up in a shipping container in their backyard, and the only fun was in socialising at the three main social gathering places for the mining residents: the Golf Club, The Recreational Club (ARC) and the bar at Bartalumba Bay. Today I am still friends with Lisa and Paul Ahrens that I met on Groote. We shared many of life's experiences including parties together and watched our small children grow.

I learned a lot about Indigenous communities while on Groote, and that influenced me later when my company offered deep discounts to Indigenous health care providers.

While there I took the time to complete my first degree through correspondence. To do so I swapped from Science to Arts. All of my subjects carried over as maths, psychology and computer science were all considered both science and arts, so I just needed to finish off a few subjects. Which I did, graduating in 1987.

It was a small community and I wanted to work so I applied for dozens of jobs. I was rejected for all of them. In 2020 I found a stack of the rejection letters and was surprised myself at the variety of work I applied for, with a number of them being technical, but alas I was not given the jobs. For each knockback I obviously just kept on trying and was eventually successfully appointed to a Timekeeper job, one that I had applied for at least three times.

On Groote I experienced a tropical cyclone and the surreal feeling of being in the eye of a cyclone. Tropical Cyclone Jason bounced around the gulf during the 1986/87 season and Groote Eylandt experienced it twice, first when it passed nearby on the eighth of February and then on the eleventh of February when it crossed Groote Eylandt itself. On both occasions the wooden floors in the house I was living in were being freshly polished with

Estapol. The howling wind, totally different blue, purple, grey colour of the sky and sea followed by the unsettling eerie silence in the eye itself is certainly a unique experience. Even now when I smell Estapol my mind and body go into a mini reaction related to the strangeness experienced in that cyclone. Peculiar for sure.

Perhaps it helped me prepare for the business storms and oddness in my future. Certainly, there was an echo of the mild panic and sudden emptiness of supermarket shelves I experienced during a cyclone and what's just happened with the Coronavirus. Human reactions are fascinating.

When I arrived on Groote there was no childcare available, except some provided to the families of the mining executives. I found that an impossible and unacceptable situation as there weren't even emergency care options. As a result, I worked hard to raise funds and establish multiple care options. I wanted childcare for my own children, so if the only way to get it was to do something about it myself, that's what I was going to do.

It felt as if the entire community got behind me, and either assisted on the committee or participated in fund raisers or both. The mining company offered a building to be the childcare centre, rent free. All I had to do was get the childcare centre licensed, set up and staffed. So I did. Funds were raised through fabulous community events such as dances, fashion parades and a mammoth effort titled "Art in the Park", where local artists displayed and sold their art works, donating profits to the childcare fund. I ploughed my way through Government funding options, childcare centre compliance paperwork and registration.

By the time I left Groote a couple of years later, due to the breakdown of my marriage, all forms of childcare were available. I played key roles in establishing the lot: after school care, long day care, emergency care and family day care. In some ways that experience introduced me to the world of Government grant applications, policies and procedures and compliance paperwork, and may have planted the seeds of ideas for my software business later.

Those who ask why there are so few women in IT have many theories, including the "leaky pipeline" where women fall out of careers at various stages along the way. At this stage of my life I was one of those women: looking after two young children and following my chef husband around the remote communities where he found work. I also found myself work when I could in some of those communities. For example in Tieri, a remote mining township in Queensland, I became a tutor in mathematics and computing; and in another remote community (Groote Eylandt) I found work as a payroll assistant for the mining company. The latter really was mostly data entry, but it was into a mainframe computer that ran the payroll and financial systems. I was fairly good at data entry and producing some reports, but found the work tediously boring and repetitive.

But then I pivoted, not because the work was boring but because it was a turbulent marriage. As the ancient saying goes, "marry in haste, repent at leisure!" I walked away from that marriage three times, including one time where with a heavy heart I even left my newborn son behind, thinking it would be too difficult for me to build a life on my own with two small children. Twice I returned to the marriage, each time hopeful it would improve, but it didn't.

That world ended with me finally leaving for good with both children.

I lost confidence in myself and my relationship decision making, especially given my record of rushing into marriage then returning multiple times to a turbulent situation. Therefore, although I left, I didn't file for divorce for almost ten years. I wanted to protect myself from ever being so foolish as to marry in haste again, and I felt being legally married would at least slow things down due to the need to get divorced first.

So there I was. I found myself a single mother of two young children, needing a way to pay for it all. I needed a well-paying career.

When I was looking at deciding on a career, there were no IT career days, no IT role models, no general information, not even many computers – so I did not have any inspiration. In the end it was this unrelated life event that resulted in me taking the steps that began my technology career.

It wasn't that I was unfamiliar with computers. I had studied computing at university – and I was hopeless at it. Though in my defense, remember my age. We are talking about the late 1970s, the era of what were known as 3GLs (third generation languages): better than what came before, but still a far cry from the much easier to understand languages and coding tools of today. Certainly not the English-like coding tools that children master today.

One thing I find amusing about this first degree, in retrospect, was my experience in computer studies in Pascal. It sounded exciting! Unfortunately, the reality proved less so. The computer hut was a giant shed, and to run a simple program we had to mark a stack of cards with a pencil then feed the cards to the computer overnight. If the cards were out of order or marked incorrectly, you never found out until the next day. I found it all too inefficient and difficult. Nor was my morale helped by being surrounded by people who wrote extra programs over and above the assignments for fun.

This all meant that I did not gain a good perception of computing. So I barely scraped through computer studies at University, and I certainly never thought I'd have a career in computing.

Hence in 1989, after leaving Groote and Clive for the final time, I found myself, nearly a decade after dropping out of university, returning to my studies – no longer a carefree single woman without responsibilities, but this time with a purpose. By then 4GLs (fourth generation languages, as you've probably guessed) had been introduced, and these promised to be easier and less frustrating. So since this tied in with my interest in mathematics, and my work with a computerised payroll system, despite my earlier experience I chose to again study computing in a post graduate degree. I also did some SQL computer coding then, which was handy later in life when my own company's chief product was mostly SQL based.

While studying for my Post-Graduate degree, something peculiar happened. I was meant to be at the college in the library studying, however instead, that day, I decided to study from home. I took Naomi to school and Thomas to his preschool kindy and returned home. After a while, I started to feel restless, though I couldn't figure out why. I couldn't put my finger on it. But I decided that even though the Kindy wasn't over, I would jump on my pushbike and head up to Tom's Kindy to pop in and observe his day.

As I arrived at the Kindy an ambulance had just pulled in and two medics jumped out, glancing over at me as I pulled up at the school gate. It all felt very strange.

I walked into the Kindy and was greeted by, "Thank goodness you're here! We've been trying to contact you at college, but no one could find you. Quick come with us!"

My heart was thumping as I was led into the next room where the medics were tending to Thomas who had a huge bump on his forehead. It was translucent and throbbing and looked frightening. I'd never seen such a giant lump before. It looked like his brain would pop out. Poor little Thomas was scared and crying, as was I by then too. We were both rushed into the ambulance. At the hospital the Xray showed that while the bump looked frightful, there was no brain damage. It would heal over time.

I sometimes think of this incident and am grateful for whatever "made" me stay at home that day so that I was able to comfort Thomas on his hospital journey. Mother's intuition at play?

Despite the topic, my purpose was not a career in IT, and at the end of that post graduate degree I applied for a job at a company called Lattice. This proved lucky for me and my future as that was my real introduction to information technology. The pivot which started with a divorce, found its final direction with a discovery. From day one, I knew it was the career for me: I discovered that I loved IT.

***

Sonja's Tips: The only way to live life is to live and experience it.

3 Climbing the Lattice

Becoming a Techie

> *Don't compromise yourself. You are all you've got —*
> *Janis Joplin*

Lattice Days

My first serious work role was at Lattice, a business branch of Mincom. My Postgraduate Diploma in Business Administration had a focus on Human Resource Management. I thought the job I applied for was a role in HR, only to discover it was for HR software. Given my later struggles with managing human resources for my own company, perhaps it was a good thing that my job was in HR software and not as an HR practitioner.

It was in this role that I discovered software technology and almost instantly fell in love with the variety of roles available and the daily challenges such work presented. I wholeheartedly plunged myself into a wide range of roles – first on the help desk/call centre, then as a trainer, then as an analyst, finally progressing to the consultant life and onto managing the professional services (consultants). I loved every single one of these jobs. I often tell this story as me "falling into IT" accidentally, where "IT bit me!".

My experience in all of those roles helped me a lot later in life. Having hands on experience across so many roles helped me know more about what sort of skills were needed when I looked for people to fill the same roles in my own company.

As a consultant I travelled a fair bit and loved it.

One trip after I had returned it was so obvious that I had had a fabulous time, most of the company started to say, "I want what Sonja just had". This was in 1989 shortly after the release of the movie "When Harry Met Sally". I had spent a week on the Atherton Tablelands in Queensland, where to my inner peace and personal delight every day after work I would spend two to five minutes driving to be rewarded by staggeringly beautiful waterfalls, alluringly tranquil lakes, or rich green national parks. I could not help but become calm and peaceful. It took at least a week for the serenity to wear off.

At first I enjoyed the thrill of exploring new places, and even just flying. Sometimes I was lucky and got the luxury of being upgraded to business class and a few times even to first class. I also got great satisfaction from feeling of value to the client, the company and to myself. It all seemed so exciting.

Once I was incredibly upgraded to the top of the top – by accident. I landed in the Philippines and in my usual style was quick to leave the plane. As I came out of Customs I was approached by some well-dressed locals. They said some name I didn't catch but then they named the hotel I was staying at, so I nodded and said yes, assuming that the hotel had made transport arrangements, a bonus surprise for me. I was taken to a stunning limousine and delivered to the hotel, where I was whisked from the foyer into a private luxurious area, spoken to extremely respectfully then escorted to the top of the hotel into a stunning penthouse suite, where I even had my own maid sitting outside the room door. I was given a tour of the facilities and the cocktail and eating area. I felt like I was in a movie. I was revelling in this star treatment.

It lasted approximately an hour.

Then came a knock on the door and a contingent of people apologising profusely. My gear was swiftly packed up and I was moved into another luxury room a floor below. The hotel had been expecting the daughter of the hotel's owner, who had arrived on the same flight, and she also was white and around my age. We white women look much the same, so they had mistaken me for her!

My new room was also stunningly gorgeous and was given to me as a "sorry we mistook you" apology. There was still a maid outside the door and she offered the added service of embossing my name on hotel stationery in gold. I took up that option.

It was a bit like that scene in *Monty Python's Life of Brian*, where the wise men shower Brian with gifts then realise he's not Jesus and take it all back.

I had many super charged trips, such as exploring the Portuguese township of Malacca when on a work trip to Malaysia that extended over a weekend. Another time I woke up in Singapore, flew to Hong Kong for a late lunch meeting, then went to sleep in Bangkok.

During one trip to the Philippines, I was staying at the company representative's home and they had arranged for their driver to take me into the city to a VIP meeting. The city traffic was horrendous. I was feeling a bit jet lagged so thought I would catch a quick nap. I glanced up and saw the time, and a short way ahead of us an intersection with a recognisable building. I dropped off to sleep and forty minutes later woke up to discover that recognisable building was now directly to my left. In that entire time of forty minutes we had travelled less than 100 metres. We arrived at my meeting late.

I had similar traffic delay experiences in Jakarta, Indonesia. Once, a colleague and I were in a taxi going to the next suburb but we were caught up in shocking traffic. It was the classic "carpark" at a standstill style, and as the car sat there and sat there, we were swarmed by street beggars. The taxi driver told us to close our eyes and not look to the right side. I was sitting on the right and soon as he told us not to look I couldn't help myself. I saw something that still lives in my memory: a young person with arms but no legs who came along on a skateboard and pushed their body onto the car, clawing their way up to my window to beg.

The taxi driver told us not to give any money, even though we were both tempted to do so. He spoke to the beggars and they moved on, but it was one of those shock moments in life that reveals a starkness about poverty. I'm surprised that I hadn't really seen it before. Maybe my life in Papua New Guinea had acclimatised me to seeing poverty? Travel for work sounds full of fun and seems fascinating, but in reality, I think it is a bit insane. As I write, I can see how crazy that type of travel actually was.

Some days when I got back to Australia from an all-night flight from Singapore, instead of going home I chose to go directly to the office for a working day. One day, upon returning from a trip on Friday morning I was advised that I was off again on Monday. As a single parent that barely gave me any time to make arrangements, let alone any time with my family.

That was when I started looking at travel differently. It was something that later in my own company I didn't want any individual to experience: I wanted individuals to have more control over their worklife travel and not to be "told".

I never made any fuss about being a single parent, and of two children to boot. It just was what it was, but I did a lot of organising behind the scenes to make sure things were in place so I was able to fully participate at work. Sometimes that caused me added stress which resulted in migraine headaches. If work meetings ran late and butted up against my absolute need to comply with childcare centre closing times, I felt extremely anxious. Not only were staff at centres very good at giving you disapproving looks and using a tone of voice that made you realise you were indeed late, but my own guilt at not being there for the kids burned strongly.

All I could do was try. I was building a life for the three of us on my own. Naomi's biological father wasn't around and Thomas's father was from a marriage I had walked away from. It was up to me alone to build a life for the kids. Years later in a business presentation, I said it felt as if I'd lost at least a decade of my life, of being just me, while I was that "struggling single parent".

When I later established my own company I never wanted anyone to go through those type of stress and anxiety levels. This made me lean towards extreme flexibility where people selected their own working hours and determined their location to work from, home, beach, in transit or wherever.

It wasn't all a struggle, in fact it only seemed so in high stress moments. In a classic Sonja move, in 1988 I spent my entire tax refund on gorgeous evening wear for both my children and myself, and took us all off for a meal on the top floor restaurant of the Sheraton Hotel in Brisbane. That evening, two special VIP guests happened to be there: the Duke and Duchess of York, Prince Andrew and Sarah Ferguson. They were seated very close to our table, and I noticed both of them glancing over. I excitedly explained to Naomi and Thomas who they were, and that added to the specialness of the evening.

Lovely music was playing, and I took my young children for a spin on the dance floor. There we were, Thomas at four in a gorgeous junior suit, and Naomi at six in a dream party dress, and me in a sparkly evening gown, laughing, spinning, obviously having a festive time together. Both of the royals got out of their seats and watched us dancing. When I sat back down, it became obvious that the royals were looking lovingly at my children. They had had their own first born in August that year but had not travelled with her to Australia, so it seemed my two children at least let them have a semi-family "intimate" moment and smile at the delight of children. To me this proved my theory that people are just people, and despite their social standing, even royals have their own yearnings and feelings, the same as us ordinary folk.

That evening was joyous for us… until the bill arrived. The restaurant had accidentally given me the royal table bill and it wasn't just for the royals: they had two tables, as their support staff accompanied them. One glance and I nearly fainted. My tax return had been good, but not that good on top of the glamourous evening wear. I frantically waved to the waiter, who after a small laugh and an apology sorted it out.

I had not yet learnt from my divorce, as my impulsiveness, or was it vulnerability, in relationships continued. I did have two affairs while at Lattice. To my amusement, or perhaps it was fright, I was once called into a work meeting where both of my ex-paramours plus one non paramour were in the small office with me. My head went wild with all sorts of comments I could make, but I had to focus on the business agenda of the meeting. I was dual tasking the business responses and all the funny lines my mind was throwing at me.

One of those affairs was really just a very short-lived one nighter, but it had been intense. A new consultant had flown in from one of the other states and we sparked instantly, so much so that that night he rushed me off my feet and into bed, literally as well as figuratively. The next day at work I was floating, only to then discover he was married. That ended the encounter for me instantly. The other man had been a secret affair, spread over a few months. That ended when he met the person he eventually married.

Outside of wild office romances, the camaraderie at Lattice was extraordinary, and I have never experienced anything like it in any workplace since. Not even in my own business, where I hired in a number of ex Lattice co-workers over the years.[iii] I even engaged three children of my Lattice co-workers over time as well.

Perhaps one thing that contributed to the overall super culture at Lattice was Martin. Martin was a legend. He was the in-house chef, who used to prepare the most delicious morning teas and lunch; his apple pie was so heavenly I am yet to find any that comes up to the same divine level. His talent with soup was renowned – especially asparagus, and also potato and leek soup. Almost everything was mouth-watering, and the dining area became a gathering ground where people mixed and mingled freely. This certainly assisted in communication and forming friendships.

In my own company, as we worked from home and worksites, I couldn't offer an onsite kitchen dining area. However, we did have meet ups and celebration events at restaurants where we feasted and laughed together.

In 1994 I worked from the Lattice Indonesian office in Jakarta, staying for almost a year. What an experience that was! The first product presentation I attended was conducted in Bahasa Indonesia, yet because it was about computers and software many of the words were already familiar, as they have no native translations and go by their English names: so to my own surprise I even partly understood the presentation.

I was living in the company's share house that was well serviced with live in staff. However, I was in for an unusual surprise when, after my first shower in the house, I stepped out of the bathtub and a giant ugly bug was waiting for me. I screamed and the head housemaid came in and laughed and laughed. It was a scorpion, a large one. They were used to scorpions, but I wasn't. That close encounter was enough for me.

Another time the head housekeeper laughed at my reaction was in my first week, when I came home from work and all the clothes that I had carelessly thrown on the bedroom floor, as I confess was my style, were gone. I thought someone had stolen them. The head housekeeper came into my room, listened, then laughed as she opened my wardrobe and showed me all the clothes, which had been washed, dried, ironed and placed in the wardrobe. I was not used to household staff and didn't even know that was part of the included services. I did, rather rapidly, get used to it though.

I also got used to going out at night. One nightclub in particular, "Tanamur", was outstanding – an incredible experience that I have never seen or experienced elsewhere. The nightclub attracted people from all walks of life, from all religions as well as atheists, street workers and shop floor assistants to executives, all mingling in the intoxicating atmosphere. People would climb up onto an elevated area and exotically and erotically dance across from one side to the other. It was an all-consuming, heady and fascinating experience. I used to take a taxi to the club then back home again as it was some distance from the house where I lived.

One Monday morning as I was heading off to work in a taxi, the driver kept sneakily looking at me through his front mirror and giggling, holding a hand to his mouth. I was confused, so asked him what he was giggling about.

"Tanamur, you Tanamur last Saturday…"

That jolted me. At that time Jakarta was a city of 13 million people, and to have a taxi driver say something like that was… well a surprise. I gulped, wondering what he was remembering, and what on earth I'd done last Saturday. He'd driven me back home after a particularly wild night at Tanamur. I had even danced along the elevated dance platform.

To accept this assignment in Jakarta, I'd had to make arrangements for my children to be cared for back in Australia. Naomi went into boarding school while Thomas temporarily went back to his father on Groote Eylandt to complete Year 5, with the plan that he would go to boarding school the following year.

In a kind gesture, Mincom flew my children to Jakarta for the Christmas and New Year holiday period. As white people in Indonesia we were targets for Santa Clauses at every location we visited, so the kids got their fill of Santa and gifts. It was starting to shape up into something magical. Getting taxis was easy: all we had to do was walk out of a shop and taxis swung by. Again, I think being a white person made us stand out as someone who probably was after a taxi. We had a sumptuous Christmas dinner and a few days stay at the Borobudur Hotel in Jakarta. After a superb time there we changed hotels to a recreational area called Ancol, where we celebrated New Year and over a few days explored the water park, Seaworld, and theme park, having a fun filled time. It was a Christmas and New Year to remember.

Naomi's birthday falls in early January, so we stayed at another luxury hotel for a weekend to celebrate that. Then shortly afterwards Thomas started feeling unwell with what appeared to be a cold or flu. He saw a doctor who provided prescription medication. By that stage I had returned to work and had hired a nanny to care for the kids during the day.

One day I returned home from work and the nanny said that Tom had been in bed most of the day. I checked in on him to discover that he was listless, his pupils were dilated, and he could not speak as his tongue was thick and fuzzy.

The house driver was away so I ran out to the street and frantically called out for a taxi to rush Tom to hospital. Usually when a taxi was required, one of the housekeepers caught a local motorbike to the main road and secured a "tourist" taxi so the driver understood English. But as none of the staff were around to do so, I ended up with a local, non-English speaking driver. In my highly-strung panic and poor Indonesian, I misspoke the name of the American hospital and the suburb it was in, so the taxi driver took off in the wrong direction.

Traffic in Jakarta is a nightmare, and it is never an easy task to turn around and change direction. It started to rain, bucketing down, when I realised we were heading the wrong way. My panic increased, and I desperately tried to explain to the driver. The heavy rain was beginning to leak through the taxi and Thomas was rapidly declining. It seemed as if he was slipping into a coma. I was wracked with worry. I started screaming in frustration, crying, and scaring the driver. It felt like a nightmare trip.

Fortunately, the driver seemed to understand my crying babble, when I told him my son was dying. He pulled over and we found someone who was able to translate what I was after, so the driver then tried some back routes and we eventually arrived at the hospital emergency department, just in the nick of time. Thomas was still alive.

It was such a fright for all of us and made me ashamed that I had only learnt a few words of the local language and had been caught out. It turned out that the medication Tom had been given for his flu consisted of two drugs that he had severe allergies to, and this was what had caused the dramatic reaction. One of those drugs was not then or now available in Australia, while the other was Chlorpheniramine Maleate, the antihistamine used in Codral Cold & Flu Night tablets. To this day he knows not to take those tablets.

As it drew closer to the start of the school year, I flew back to Brisbane with my two children to ready them for boarding school. It was to be a two week trip for me, but while there two things happened to change those plans.

The first was I was asked to look in on one of Lattice strategic projects, as they felt it wasn't running as smoothly as it ought to. I did that and it was agreed that I stay a couple more weeks to assist its implementation. Three months later I flagged to my Mincom manager that I was living out of a suitcase on two weeks clothing. Their simple reply was "OK we will get your gear in Indonesia packed up and shipped back for you. We need you here."

The second incident was that due to his very young age Tom was having issues settling into the boarding school, and it was decided by both the school and me that it was best for him to return home to regular school. Luckily for him and me those work circumstances meant I was then staying in Brisbane. Unluckily for me the changed timing of my work in Indonesia had meant that I was a few weeks short of being able to claim nontaxable status for my time in Indonesia, so I ended up paying both Indonesian and Australian tax for my work there.

Despite the sometimes stressful moments, the interesting and fun times were in abundance. I remember those Lattice days with great fondness, and I carry with me deep friendship and respect for many I worked with while there, especially you, Enid and Peter. I believe it was there I first became aware of and worked with the wide range of personalities that are drawn to the technology sector. And it was where I got to fine tune my communication style.

Many years later, I visited a client who occupied the same building in Brisbane where Lattice was housed during the first few years I worked there. The outside had been spruced up, but the interior was eerily similar. A flood of happy memories took me by surprise, and I had to explain to the client what was going on with me as I stood gazing around with a silly grin.

My life experiences have helped me realise that it's not worth getting stressed if things don't work out exactly according to your plan. Everything we experience contributes to who we are and what we do, and what feels like a disaster at the time, might be what changes your life for the better. At some stage of your life almost everything you have gone through or experienced comes together, you hit the sweet spot and your life's burning passion flame ignites. These experiences can form life's aha moments!

***

Sonja's Tips: Don't settle for anything less than yourself.
Only you are you, so be you.

Dad (right) and a work crew colleague on their way to Australia from Hamburg, Germany. They travelled on the SS Sydney, pictured in the background docked into Colombo (Sri Lanka) on 7 October 1951

(below) Dad and his thrilling motorbike

Circa 1955 - (left) Dad looking mysteriously Bad Boy

Photo credit - The Trove Project

1955- Mum and Dad courting in George Town Photo credit - Ray and Jackie Piper

Left- My arrival. Back- Dad and Mum. Front from L-R- Me (b. 1959), Brother Paul (b.1956) and brother Peter (b.1957). Loving the way my face is so fiercely looking out at the world.

My Parents – married Photo credit- The Trove

I am almost eight in this photo. It is in the backyard of our Georgetown home, with our cubbby house visible in the background. Mum and brother Peter in the backrow, myself and sister Susan (b. 1960) in the front.

1969 I remember those Encyclopaedia Britannica books so well. The TV was of course Black and White. Photos Credit - Trove Project.

1969 Sarah (b. 1966), Susan, myself, Peter and Dad. Paul was away at Geelong Grammar School. The Mercedes is visible in the background of the outside shot.

1978- In Germany- Back- Aunt Gudren, My grandparents Oma and Opa with my parents. Front- Cousin Antje and youngest sister Sarah.

Circa 1973_'74- In Zeehan Back L to R- Peter (had joined the navy), Dad, Paul. Front Susan, Sarah and me.

Circa mid 1970's- Port Moresby view towards Paga Hill with Hanuabada in mid view.

Circa mid 1970's- Port Moresby. Our house in Gerehu Stage 1.

Circa 1970's- Zeehan Main Street The Gaiety Theatre.

1976- At St Anne's School Townsville – now the Cathedral School. L to R- Kathy Bogiatsis (day Captain), Sister Chaseley, Liz Mitchell (sports Captain), and me (Boarding Captain).

2000- The Bernhardt family years later at Sarah's wedding. L to R- Paul, Susan, Mum, Sarah, Dad, Me, Peter.

2020- New Years Eve The family on Ovation of The Seas Back L to R- me, Paul, Peter Middle mum Front Sue, Sarah Dad died in 2010.

Circa 1978- A University Event at Brisbane Town Hall. L to R- Lorraine Prior, myself, Sue Rennick.

2018- Jane Thomason and I holding up the first book we were both named authors.

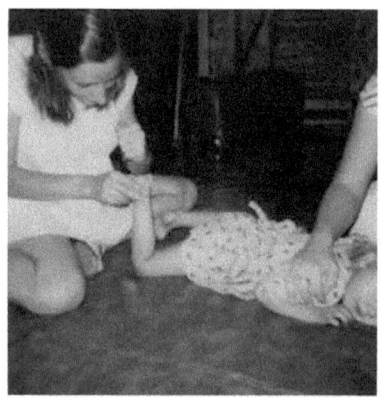
4 Me doing CP Heel Pounding exercise on Naomi, with the Physio from the Spastic Centre observing.

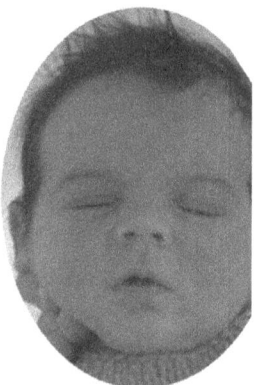
1984- When Thomas was 3 days old we packed up and to Tieri in Central Queensland. Our home was a caravan

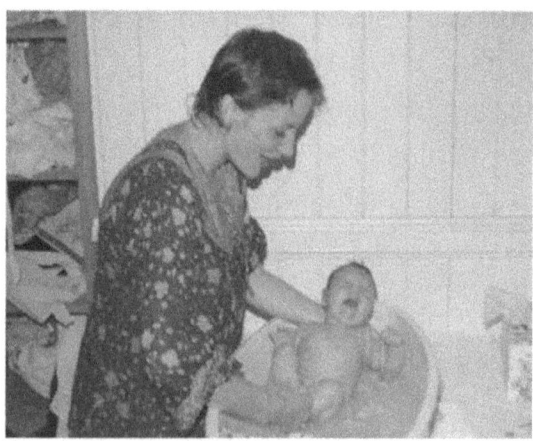
1982- I was living in a share house, a lovely large old Queenslander in Toowong, so converted part of my bedroom into the baby's area.

Girls Do IT Too

At a hens party on Groote, I'm front row middle.

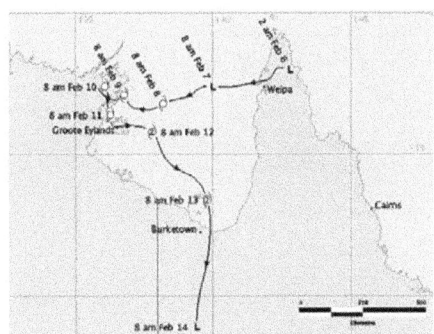

TC Jason 1986_87 season path by Australian Government Department of Meteorology.

Circa 1989- Both Tom and Naomi heading off for holidays to visit Clive.

Circa 1992 Naomi, me as Easter Bunny and Tom. I dived into fund aising for the Spastic Centre, running car raffles at shopping centres and on this particular Easter I was Easter Bunny visiting a range of child care centres.

Roger, Kylie, Noel, Doug, Sitting Robin (not my husband), Lynette

Lynelle, Peter, David's wife, David, Roland.

Girls Do IT Too

Saint Nick- Lattice Xmas Party Me with Santa (Nick Brooking). Nick was a payroll software guru. I learnt lots from Nick about software implementations.

We even partied outside of work. (Lynelle, Peter and me). This is a party at the home of my friend Helen from my Post Graduate Diploma days

Jakarta Indonesia- Tanamur. Photo by Joe Mud PS 10,000 rupiah was about AU$1.

The Socialising

Girls Do IT Too

4 WIT's Birth and Almost a Funeral
To Wit

We all live in suspense, from day to day, from hour to hour; in other words, we are the hero of our own story –
Mary McCarthy

Almost a Funeral

It was late 1996, when I suffered a life-threatening bout of Meningococcal Meningitis. As I lay in my hospital bed recovering, I started thinking about all the fascinating women I knew who were involved in technology, who didn't know each other or even about each other, yet. I promised myself that on recovery I would do something about it.

And I did. In 1997 I kicked off the action that resulted in Women in Technology (Qld) being created, and I served as its inaugural President from 1997 to 1999. WiT remains alive and healthy in 2020 and has grown to be a highly respected industry association. There is an immense sense of pride to have conceived and birthed that baby.

At that time, I was living in Runcorn in a rental house next door to my parents' home. Early in the morning they dropped over to say goodbye as they were heading off to Townsville on a holiday. I was lying in bed feeling sick. I knew I was really, really ill, as during the night I had gone through bouts of passing out and then waking up, only to pass out again before I could get up to call an ambulance. I didn't want to alarm my parents, so I put on a brave face and even when Mum asked if she should stay back to look after me, I said no and encouraged them to still go on their break.

Almost as soon as Mum and Dad left, I dragged myself out of bed and went to call an ambulance. As I listened to the message urging people to only call an ambulance if it was an absolute emergency, I decided to call a taxi instead. Little did I know that I was definitely an absolute emergency.

I arrived at the Emergency Department of Princess Alexandria hospital in Brisbane and was fairly rapidly triaged, though then I had to sit and wait. While sitting waiting on the hard plastic chairs, a mysterious rash started forming across my body and my neck began to feel stiff. When a nurse saw the rash, I was suddenly moved into a private room and a group of doctors and nurses surrounded me. By that stage the hospital lights had started to hurt my eyes, so I closed them and kept them covered.

The combination of the rash, stiff neck and light sensitivity rang loud bells with the hospital staff and I was immediately admitted to the infectious disease ward.

Mum and Dad's holiday wasn't exactly relaxing, as within two days of their arrival, Townsville radio was blasting out a health warning asking for Tom and Olive Bernhardt to urgently call into Queensland Health for an infectious disease caution and check in. Not the relaxing break they'd hoped for.

When I contracted Meningococcal Meningitis, it was around Brisbane Ekka (show) time and there were reports that some people had died of the disease. As a result, the media was interested in interviewing me when I recovered. The TV clip featured me and Dad (home from his Townsville getaway) walking side by side down the footpath chatting – with an overlay of the death statistics then the announcement, "but this woman survived": followed by an interview with me discussing the massive amount of drugs that the infectious diseases ward had injected into me, the incredible body pains, the "death" rash and the terrible weakness (I couldn't even squeeze a shampoo bottle). Funny on reflection how at that time I was rather concerned about not being able to squeeze tooth paste or shampoo. It reminds me of when as a child when my main concern on seeing broken dining room chairs was to worry about where was I to sit to eat breakfast.

Did I feel lucky I survived? Probably.

But to me at the time I was more focused on full recovery and getting life back on track. I was a single parent of two children plus I had work responsibilities to look after. I felt a pressing need to get back and into IT.

My Lattice workplace was shocked to discover that what I'd originally thought was the flu was a deadly infectious disease that put me in hospital.

Three people from work featured highly during that time. One, Lorelle Turner, who had medical training, was fascinated by the infection as she used to work in a lab that identified the disease and she knew the potentially deadly implications. My boss, Grahame Neilson, was so concerned that he was granted permission to visit me in hospital, suitably cleansed and attired in special infectious disease gear.

As I lay in my hospital bed speaking with him and beginning to respond to his concerns, for the first time I started to worry about my mortality. Another colleague, Aston Bell, who lived geographically close to me, became a courier between work and myself during my months of recovery. In his words, "You being you, still wanted to keep busy and involved. There was no Skype, Zoom or WebEx back then, so I was the daily courier of files, folders, disks and information back and forth. Drop offs and pick-ups were like today's COVID social distancing, where I had to stand at the fence or away from the house to speak with you and we had a system of where to place the files etc."

Another of my close work colleagues, Peter Kaandorp, said to me at the time, "You rarely crash Sonja, but when you do, boy do you crash!"

And he was right, throughout life I rarely did crash or drop out, and when I did it was only ever for significant dramatic things. It took a few months to get fully back on track but hey, this woman survived.

Women In Technology

As I mentioned earlier it was my brush with death that inspired the formation of the Women in Technology organisation (WIT) – an important moment for me and my community engagement.

WIT (later rebranded to WiT) was launched at the Brisbane Polo Club in 1997, at that stage one of the only clubs in Brisbane that "allowed" women entry. The launch speaker was Jo Sherman, a lawyer with great technical competence and interests who went on to develop software for the legal system. Aston, a work colleague at that time, describes it in this way: "I recall attending the first ever WIT seminar that you organised. You had passion about this concept, tried to market it to through the industry and had no idea how many people would turn up. Boom, the venue was a full house, and the rest is history."

I have many WIT memories, worthy of a book of their own, but a standout memory was WIT's first Christmas event. It was held at the Stamford Plaza in the relaxing garden area. Joan Sheldon, then Deputy Premier, attended the event. Her aide later told me that she was very tired and hadn't wanted to come, though duty meant she needed to. As it turned out she had an extraordinary time and thoroughly enjoyed it, staying longer than she had intended. One of the triggers for her enjoyment was when, as I was explaining what WIT was about, I took the stage and said "What is WIT? … apart from a wonderful quality to have in a partner… WIT is…" One of the male attendees, from Microsoft, called out to ask if he could be a member, and I threw back that, "We welcome half-wits" … and we progressed from there.

I also announced, to the surprise of the WIT board, that we were launching a scholarship. This announcement was greeted with spontaneous gifts from the crowd. Many companies donated items for the scholarship. Apple donated a computer. Microsoft donated software. As I jumped back on the stage with pure joy to tell everyone of those gifts, others called out donating more to add to the scholarship. It was a great way to demonstrate a technology community coming together – a very warm collegiate technology atmosphere of working together and having fun to boot.

The WiT Awards are now a backbone of the organisation. They have grown to span dozens of categories and are highly respected across Australia.

Dale Spender, are you there?

As I need to confess something to you. Dale was scheduled as the guest speaker at a WIT event. I had not met Dale at that stage but had read her profile: "Dale Spender is an Australian feminist scholar, teacher, writer and … Spender draws parallels with how derogatory terms are used to maintain racism". Well I was terrified. I was so afraid that she might say something overly controversial and that WIT might face an unfavourable incident, I was literally shaking.

On reflection I may have been scared by the use of the word "feminist". It took me decades to realise that my own intervention activities and interests clearly demonstrated that I was a feminist. I had never thought of myself as one, nor labelled myself as such, but perhaps actions speak louder than labels. Though "feminist" can mean many things, and what I do know is I was an individual doing things to help empower other women.

Dale of course turned out to be magnificent, and so interesting that we formed a friendship and went on to do a lot of activities together. I've even been privileged to visit her at her home and view her famous purple wardrobe. I recall buying Dale purple pasta in Italy one year. I was delighted to discover it in a small shop in Florence. I am sure the shop owner thought I was a little overexcited about pasta. My enthusiasm shone through regardless of language.

Dale always presented with perfectly coiffed hair, so on one occasion during a break while judging WIT awards one year, I asked Dale for advice on my greying hair and how to manage it. "Should I just let it grow, or keep dyeing it?"

She said, "Darling, one never *lets* their hair just go grey!" Then she went on to outline a process to undertake.

In a mini confession, sorry Dale: I ended up just letting mine go grey.

In fact, in 2011 I entered the "Greatest Shave in the World" event where, in a perhaps overly theatrical bid to get off the hair dyeing roundabout, I had a full head shave (with the first cut by footballer Shane Webcke)[iv]. It was not just a way to get a cheap celebrity haircut, I did have the additional motivation of raising the much-needed funds for cancer research. Even though I only registered a few weeks before the "cut-off" date, thanks to my deep technology corporate connections I ended up being highest individual fund raiser in the technology sector in Queensland. My target was to raise $10,429 – because $10,000 is a nice round figure; 42 is, well, you know, the "meaning of life"; and 9 is a mathematically "magic" number I always enjoyed as a child. I didn't quite get there but came very close. The shave also achieved a fresh hair restart for me, so it was of double benefit. A journalist for the Courier Mail had a cartoon created of me in the shave, and it made me laugh as it was a rather accurate caricature. I still have that picture in my office today.

This book is not about WIT: it has its own tale to tell. But I do want to cover the steps from the trigger to create WIT to its actual beginning. Earlier, I revealed how in 1996 my near death experience resulted in me promising to bring together women in tech. Two events in early 1997 reminded me of my promise.

The first was when I attended an Australian Information Industries Association (AIIA) networking event and felt overwhelmed by the number of males in suits. There was a sea of mostly dark suits, in Queensland which is bit irrational given the warm weather. Being short, it seemed like I was surrounded by a huge dark, stormy cloud. That made me think it would be less intimidating to attend if there were other visible women present, or maybe even other shorter people!

The second spur to action was a woman, Jane Reid, who popped in and out of my life over a few years. Jane called me in April 1997 to arrange a lunch catch up. Immediately on returning from that lunch I was fired up, I ran back to work, determined to make my idea about connecting all the women in IT happen.

I called the IIB (Information Industries Bureau) where the director, Brian Cordiner, told me that just the night before their CEO, Liz Manning, had assigned funds at a meeting specifically to assist women in technology. I had struck gold, almost literally, and WIT was born.

I contacted the IIB because earlier, in 1993, I'd held a job role that opened up the IT world for me – at the IIB itself, or at least its predecessor, the then newly formed Queensland Government Information Industries Board. In that role I got out and about to assess Technology firms and assist with completing grant applications to aid their growth. Doing those assessments I learnt heaps, met many, many people, and got to work with some people I still fondly remember, such as Greg Williams, David Henderson and Karin Eisele. David popped in and out of my life over time, as he pursued a career in investment and as chairman of numerous organisations. Karin mastered the world of marketing, and thanks to social media we reconnected after a few decades. So I was aware of the IIB's spread and impact. By 1997 it had reformed as the Bureau, with a similar charter to the Board I had worked at, so it was natural that I reached out to it.

The IIB pulled together our initial group of people[v] and granted us funds of $5,000. And with that we began the WIT journey on baby legs.

Over time I've lost contact with some of the original members, however I remain in contact with Ann Uldridge, Sonya Trau and Jenny Beresford. The 20th anniversary brought me back in touch with Bernadette Hyland and Glenda Slingsby, both of whom achieved great successes overseas.

The interest in the "issue" of women in information technology grew from those beginnings and featured in other organisations. In September 1999 the Australian Computer Society (ACS) held a Women in Information Technology seminar at the Mercure Hotel. I was delighted to be a presenter, along with well-known Queensland identities.[vi] One of the presenters, Wayne Bucklar, was a humorous fellow, and he later invited me to present in at least two annual technology debates in Far North Queensland, that were super fun. At one of them I dressed up as a mermaid. I don't recall why, but I am sure it was entirely relevant to what I had to say about technology.

Today, as many would know, the issue of the lack of females in technology is having a second wave, or maybe a third, with significant uptake in projects, programs and sponsorships as well as overall awareness. In 2020 there is a plethora of organisations, support and programs. Back then, WIT was about it, and we designed and implemented a wide range of projects and programs for role modelling, mentoring, career days, board readiness, busines matching and awareness raising.

WIT became a significant influence on me through the people I met, and the many programs I was involved in designing and implementing. These tuned my project planning and implementation skills, and my overall sector focus. I also put into action other promises I'd made to myself during recovery. Those promises were to buy my own home and find a partner. I'd been a single mum for over a decade by that stage.

Nothing like a brush with death to help clear the brain cobwebs and reshape your life.

Finding Love

It might have taken me over a decade and two starts to find a career, but I am also capable of snap decisions. Buying a house happened much to the amusement of the sales person.

I was recovering from my bout with meningococcal meningitis at home in a rental property, when a real estate salesperson knocked on my door. He did their usual high level generic presentation, and I said, "OK I'll buy a house."

His jaw dropped open in shock at such an enthusiastic and positive "I'll buy" statement after a one time only, short generic presentation. Little did he know my circumstances and promise to myself. In some ways it is a classic example of both of us being in the right place at the right time.

I am not one to believe in fate, I am more of a fate is what you make it person, however…

Finding love took a little longer and a fair few additional "presentations".

I wasn't really sure where to start. With the exception of a few wild years in Perth with my best friend Lorraine, and my infamous times at Tanamur in Jakarta, I am not really a night club person. I also hadn't spotted any likely husband candidates for me through my work contacts: lots of colleagues and friends but no love interests.

So I floundered for a while. There was stark reminder of my promise to myself when I attended Jane Reid's fortieth birthday party. The party was made up of 79 people, 39 couples and me. That rang a loud bell.

It wasn't until a few of us from WIT took a table at an evening business event that the way to go about finding myself a new partner became obvious. At that table were myself, Sonya D'Aoust and Glenda Slingsby. Glenda was accompanied by a charming, good looking fellow. Later, in the ladies' powder room, I said to Glenda "Matt's nice…"

She gushed "Oh isn't he! You'll never guess how I met him. An internet dating website called RSVP."

That sealed the deal for me. That night when I got home, I checked out RSVP and registered.

It turns out that evening was pivotal for Sonya D'Aoust as well. While Matt Trau was a gentleman with Glenda, the chemistry between him and Sonya was sparklingly obvious. They went on to marry and have children and remain married today.

You never know who you meet, when. So much of life requires careful planning. But so much can also depend on luck. I think the same mix of luck and planning applies to businesses and success.

I had fun on the RSVP dating web site, as I registered two profiles. The profiles and what I said were the same, but I gave them different names, one a "fun sexy name" and the other a more serious stylish name. I did this on purpose as it helped me "trap" and easily rule out people who just blasted anyone and everyone without any discretion. I also tended to rule out those attracted to my sexy fun profile name. That made the task of trimming the possibilities far easier for me.

I learnt a lot from that internet dating experience. Communicating electronically does let you meet at an intellectual and sense of humour level before getting confused by any of the body attraction aspects. But it is **not** the entire package. More than once I got on famously with someone's written words but when we physically met there was no chemistry. Nothing at all going on. Some said, "Let's remain friends," but I always replied, "Sorry, not in this for friends, I have enough of those for now. I'm after a partner so it's goodbye from me."

Then along came Robin. On the first night we met at the Thai Orchid restaurant in Springwood, Brisbane, my happy reaction scared me so much that when dinner was over, I ran to my car actually a little afraid. Mind you, it didn't start that way.

With my Germanic sense of timing I'd arrived at the restaurant early, so was already seated and with a view of the reception area. When Robin arrived, I thought *"Please don't let it be him, don't let it be him."* In my judgemental way, I had rapidly judged him on his unfashionable clothing.

Anyway, it was him, and he turned out fabulous. In truth, he was a bit of a beast. He, a philosopher and scientist, gave me a philosophical, ethical and moral puzzle to do…. on our first date. Luckily for my future amazing life, I passed, proving we were philosophically compatible. With puzzles like that, the common wisdom is to say there is no right answer: but the real "right answer" is in how much *your* answer says about your own values, ethics and philosophy of life.

Robin and I married in March 1999, just after I was made redundant from Mincom. I had the time to do it, so we did. These were the early days of internet dating, and the *Courier Mail* ran a page three story on my internet romance, titled "Sonya nets her perfect match in cyberspace." They misspelt my name but they got the rest correct.

We had our delightful daughter Kira in May 2003. I was 44 years old and it had been 19 years since I'd last had children. That was a bit of fun – not. I was anticipating something as quick and easy as my first two births. Multiple pain killer methods and twelve hours later, I was less confident. The "muscle memory" of childbirth did not seem to be there 19 years later! With that experience, I changed my opinion about women being wussy and complaining about childbirth and pain: I had come to understand what it was all about.

***

Sonja's Tip: You are responsible for your life. If you want things to change take action.

5 Networking Madness

Making Connections, Gaining Visibility

Adventure is worthwhile in itself – Amelia Earhart

Who said people in IT were nerds with no social life?

Exciting and extremely busy times full of a whirlwind of networking events and social occasions carried me along for years. In amongst the classic time wasting and time wasters there were also a large number of collegiate connections and activities. I wholeheartedly volunteered for so many industry activities. At one stage I used my maths and tech background to develop an algorithm to calculate how much time I voluntarily "gave away". I was shocked to discover that three quarters of my weekend time was consistently spent on volunteer activity, and I in-kind contributed and physically spent one quarter of my income on my voluntary involvement. Good thing I'm not into sport or other weekend hobbies, otherwise I could not have done it. In reality my volunteer involvement became both my sport and hobby. Life in technology and specifically as a woman in technology became my burning passion.

The things we do for that internal fire that drives you on and on!

Tech Glory Days in Queensland

Queensland IT in the mid/late 90s up to 2004 was the glory era. The era when the sky was the limit and the result was grand events, innovation showcases, significant cross company networking, regional tours, media stories, and amazing Christmas parties. All with no borders or barriers, instead with an industry that worked together to build the overall sector. I'm sure that even introverts could not have helped but become involved during that era.

Today the Australian Information Industries Association (AIIA) run their iAwards, whose winners are promoted to the Asia Pacific ICT Awards (APICTA). However, this did not start with AIIA: it began in Queensland IT long before.

Paul Phillips was the mastermind behind APICTA, and in my experience Queensland has never since seen the incredible IT buzz, media interest, activity, networking and innovation showcasing that resulted from APICTA. Paul had a knack for attracting incredibly good-looking female staff. At one stage my husband commented that each new hire seemed even better looking than the previous one. My husband knew he was "safe" making the comment and wouldn't get in trouble from me for daring to notice attractive females, because it was simply a statement of fact. Besides, I had noticed it myself. I asked Paul about this and he laughed saying he let the "girls" make the selection, so it wasn't his doing. Extremely good looking they may have been, but their dedicated work and talent was equally as obvious. It was no easy role to run those awards.

My own role in this was originally as a judge and member of the APICTA Advisory Board. Later I was appointed deputy chair plus overall chair of the Australian judging panels, and an international judge. All of this on an unpaid voluntary basis. I rapidly became enchanted with the intense networking across all levels of the Queensland's IT stage (multinationals, corporates, SMEs, individuals, educators and Government). I was relatively new to a tech career in Queensland, yet, thanks to APICTA, I was exposed to and gained exposure across all tiers. With many others regularly mingled and shared jokes with CEOs and General Managers of firms such as Oracle, Unisys, GBST, Optus, and Apple. Even those people who were more standoffish and bristly joined the activities and the barbs were exchanged in a friendly atmosphere.

One of my own detractors at that time was Wayne (I genuinely forget his surname), who headed up AAPT. Wayne and I used to throw "friendly" insults to each other at group gatherings. It is not surprising that a loud female publicly standing up to someone used to more respectful deference helped fuel such exchanges. In my normal manner I just treated him at face value, ignoring that he had such an important, powerful role and was politically connected. In the end people are people; roles may change, but the person is how they present and behave, and my natural instinct is to respond to the person, not their position.

I received a great growth experience through this whole involvement – nature's own mentoring – without a structured program, organically grown out of industry buzz, passion and a common goal.

When I was chair of the overall judging panels for APICTA, this meant appointing, matching and training over 130 individuals from a wide variety of organisations across multiple award categories. The most memorable parts of my involvement were the incredible collegiate networking events held as part of the APICTA process, and the ease of meeting, mixing and enjoying the company of such a vibrant IT community. We had APICTA general events and judges' training and mentoring events, cocktail evenings, lunches and more. My wardrobe is still packed with all the glamorous gowns and accessories I purchased during that time. Not that I fit many of them anymore, especially post Coronavirus lockdown.

APICTA contributed a real sense of community and pride in technology innovation to the Queensland tech scene. The Innovation Showcases, from school children through to multi nationals, were fascinating to attend and showcased all the award nominees from across the state. It was exciting to see and learn about what was developed and being developed at the coal face and the motivations behind each creation.

APICTA regional tours were an experience, often kangaroo flight hopping between regional townships such as Mackay, Rockhampton, Townsville and Cairns. On tour tech presentations were held to spread the news about IT, and the awards were promoted at schools and technology businesses, and a lot of genuine friendships were formed.

Cairns always played a big part in these tours: it was the big city versus the smaller townships we visited. I loved flying into Cairns, with the sweeping views of the ocean, the beach and mountains all in one glance. It was almost as if peace descended on me as I admired the view. Perhaps the tropical look and feel brought memories of Papua New Guinea back to me.

Cairns was where I first encountered the talented Kathleen Priestly, an educator and an early adopter of technology in schools. I recall their award application "Airport but no Planes", which was all about establishing an Apple Airport WiFi network across her school, which back then was bleeding edge. I always found the innovation and application of technology from other viewpoints that we saw in the awards fascinating and energising.

In each township the media came out in force, with radio, print and television. In smaller towns – our visits were a highlight. At that time, I was already presenting on ABC radio and often popped into the regional town ABC studio for a small technology session, about APICTA or WIT or IT in general.

In one of those regional radio sessions, I was asked about the value of attending university and its relationship to technology careers. With apology to any associations I have with universities, in my usual outspoken way I stated that technology moved so fast it was better to cultivate a talent for rapid change and learning new things rather than going through years of formal studies. When technology churns faster than the three to four year timeframe of a degree (not to mention the timeframe of developing the courses in the first place), you might find yourself a well-qualified expert on outdated technology. I did continue on to say University will teach a person discipline and frameworks which have some value, but ultimately, I thought short courses and hands on experience in a job was best.

I recall some tour occasions fondly.

Once when in Cairns, in a typical Sonja act of either bravery or treating people as just people, I sat down at breakfast next to Terry Mackenroth (recently appointed technology minister). Mackenroth certainly knew how to keep a conversation on the track he wants it to follow and didn't put up with any rubbish. I started to discuss the "issue" of the lack of visibility of women in technology and he threw some questions at me, that I responded to rapid-fire. The next thing I knew, on our return to Brisbane Mackenroth had set in place steps to create a Ministerial Technology Advisory Council and had sent out a call insisting that each invitee include at least one female applicant. I served on that council through three technology ministers from 1998-2004: Terry Mackenroth, Paul Lucas and Chris Cummings.

On another occasion, at a Townsville event, two parallel streams were running – one was the formal awards event, including meeting the minister, the other was a gathering for those with an interest in women in technology. Ross McLeish, Executive at Optus/Singtel, recalls that the tour group was fascinated to observe that the women in tech event attracted three times the number of attendees that the official event did.

On one kangaroo hop flight, I was seated next to a gentleman who was not part of the tour group – usually we took up every seat of the small plane. On this occasion there were a couple of other passengers. When the flight stopped briefly, the gentleman got off the plane, while those going to the next stop remained on board. The booming voice of Terry Mackenroth called through the plane, "He wasn't scheduled to get off here, but he has been next to Sonja talking the entire, way and had to escape!" The entire plane, including myself, had a great belly laugh. It demonstrated the comradeship that APICTA bought to the technology scene in Queensland. My mum's prediction about me talking rang true again!

I was once privileged to be seated next to Professor Peter Poole on a Brisbane to Cairns leg of an APICTA tour. Peter was very interesting and I spent the trip questioning him about his life and listening with great interest. Among his many achievements he did pioneering work on SILLIAC and

CSIRAC (early electronic computers) and worked with Professor Harry Messel at Sydney University and then again later at Bond University. When I met Peter he was actively engaged in the SETI project (the Search for Extra Terrestrial Intelligence). Peter was inducted into the ACS Pearcey Hall of Fame in 2010 (I was inducted into the same Hall of Fame in 2019).

Peter remarked to me a few years later that at first he thought, "Oh what have I got into, this woman talks and talks." Then he started enjoying our conversation, saw that I was a decent person, and we began our friendship.

I was delighted to be invited to his 80th birthday party in 2011. Peter sadly died in 2017. He was a true gentleman, smart and kind.

Meet Me For Coffee?

Events that on reflection I believe I was crazy to keep doing were early morning breakfast events – industry, school talks, generic business. These were mostly held in Brisbane, which meant I needed to catch a 5:30am train, from the Gold Coast, to get to an event on time, especially if I was a speaker. Those out of Brisbane city I drove to, however they still required very early morning starts. Luckily I am a morning person, so at the time I felt I was thriving in this environment. It was certainly energising for me, and I hear it was for others too.

I spent a number of years of breakfasts where I would stand at networking tables, waiting for the minister's arrival. It all seemed thrilling. I accepted each opportunity with enthusiasm even though often I was the token female. Me, being me, made sure that my voice was heard at each table I sat at.

When your head starts to poke out and your name is thrown around town and in the media, another phenomenon happens. So many times, too many times, people want to grab a coffee and a chat with you. They then proceed to ask for your help with one of their issues. It happened to me often, until in the end I was coffeed and chatted out. It's ironic because it coincides with when you are most busy, and this "meet me for coffee" game is a big time stealer, and often IP advice stealer.

I vividly recall initially being so thrilled at anyone asking to meet with me that I accepted all invitations. In my ignorance I let the asker set the place and time, which meant I spent a number of years frantically running from coffee shop to coffee shop across town.

My Germanic heritage meant I am a stickler for time, and to me it was nearly a sin to be late, even being on time I considered late. Arriving early is a must for those meeting me and also for myself, hence my crazy running between meetings so that I was never late. One would think I got fit due to that, but alas the coffee shop eats and drinks made sure I didn't.

I don't even like coffee.

BuziWomen

Busy, Busy, Busy.

Parallel to the industry networking and running my small business I also launched into a web-based travel advice business. This was before Trip Advisor's global spread and was called Buziwomen.com. It was specifically designed for female business travellers, providing multimedia information, hints and tips on local languages, customs, expectations and safety.

I was attending a mentoring event where mentors and mentees took to the stage and told their stories. One of the mentors was a fascinating, powerful businesswoman named Adrienne Ward. I was very impressed with Adrienne and what she had to say. I wasn't the only one impressed with her, as after the event she had a string of people wanting to meet her. So I decided that instead of waiting in the queue I would track down her details and make contact later.

Adrienne responded to my message, and we met face to face. She swept me up in her world, and even interviewed me on a television show she was producing. Adrienne and I bounced ideas off each other, and the concept of a site for women business travellers was born. We jointly founded the Intellcorp company, which gathered some private investors and launched the BuziWomen web site. To our excitement we even had some stunning billboards displayed near airports.

Adrienne was full of energy and ideas, knew many people, and also knew the steps we needed to take to get the idea up and running. We engaged a company to develop the website, and in a typical techie tale it was developed in the funkiest language at that time, ColdFusion, and could only be updated by using the developing company. Something very limiting for a site we wanted to continually update. Today ColdFusion is part of the Adobe suite; back then it was the new big thing, and the majority of our investors' capital was sadly spent on developing that site.

The idea was great, and the future success of Trip Advisor proved that there was a place for such a concept. However we failed to get to a critical mass of users before the capital ran out, and we sadly folded.

My respect for, and friendship with, Adrienne endured.

Through Adrienne I met a young businesswoman who I felt would get on really well with another young businesswoman I knew, so I introduced them to each other, saying I expected they could do business together. Well, three things happened: they did get on like the proverbial house on fire; they did set up a business that apparently had a revenue of $1.3 million in its first three months of operations; and I wished I'd asked for a commission.

One of the many tips Adrienne taught was there is value in having some professional photographs at your fingertips, so when asked to provide one for media stories you are both happy with the result and also don't have to scramble to find one.

Going Up in The World

In my hands was a gorgeous looking embossed personal invitation to the Premier's Christmas Party. My name was on that invitation, it was mine. How I remember the excitement that first time to the Annual Christmas Bash on the Speaker's Green at Parliament House in Brisbane. Oh, how on my walk from the Central Train Station, I felt so special, so honoured, so proud. I chose to take the train up and back as I expected to be drinking, hopefully some decent wine, so didn't want to drive.

As I strutted towards Parliament House, I ran into some industry colleagues[vii] heading to the same event. They were "old hats" and knew what was in store. To me it was fresh and exciting, plus I was secretly thrilled at walking and chatting with them, both State General Managers of major tech firms and me, just me… a little girl with her own very small tech company.

The place to me was buzzing. So, so many people, so many "players", so much happening. I almost felt lost. I discovered good food and readily flowing wine that was drinkable, which was a bonus as I had discovered that often at networking events the quality of the wine is poor. In my newbie innocence I felt that the political speeches were interesting, and I clapped and cheered.

Once the Premier's Xmas Party was on a day I was flying back into Brisbane after a business trip. All I wanted to do was go home, but my husband encouraged me to attend. I did, and I did enjoy it. By that stage I was across the political platform and was able to tune out what I didn't need to hear again, and just network and catch up. And eat and drink!

I certainly did meet more than a handful of up and coming politicians at these events. A number of whom later were appointed to ministerial portfolios, some even to the top job. I'm not sure if there is a little thrill in that for me or not. It was never anything I experienced an advantage from, it was just what it was, time passing and people career climbing.

It was quite a different scene for me a number of years later when I started to choose not to attend the events. By then I was aware that they were mostly just a political platform, with messages where I had "heard it before"; plus in my opinion many people there had a hidden agenda. Eventually as my Brisbane "presence" reduced, I was dropped off the invitation list. However, I had my prime time there, practicing my unique (sounds better than "pushy"!) networking style of poking my way into a circle of conversation and attempting to contribute.

Too many Johns

At one stage my life seemed full of Johns...

John Grant (Data #3, CEO), John Puttick (GBST, founder and chair), John Vickers (Unisys, General Manager and CEO) plus there was Jon Uldridge (who sadly died from cancer in 2007. His funeral was one public occasion when I freely cried and cried).

In my opinion all my Johns were nice guys. Welcoming, intelligent, interesting and they all treated me with respect at every interaction. I was proud to know them and to know that they actively engaged in discussions with me. Another fellow in the same category of nice guy, not a John but I'll include him with them, is Rob Holloway (MD of Optus).

I really should have staged a photo with me and my Johns. I did bump into John Grant in 2019 and made sure I got a photo.

Socialising on a Grand Scale

Back in those days, tech corporates took out corporate enclosures for the Gold Coast Indy Grand Prix (later this became Formula 1, then the Surfers Paradise Street Circuit). On at least two years that I attended, the penthouse suite of the Surfers Paradise International Hotel was a venue where technology personalities gathered and watched the race, with 360 degree views of the race track and even a close view of a fighter jet as it flew over. This was a great opportunity to cover business links and leads in a social manner and to keep up to date with technology progress. And like most work and sports mixing, a bonding opportunity.

In other years, I was a guest of the HP and the Oracle boxes/enclosures, where the atmosphere was super charged and there was a real sense of a tech community. To this day I still have my HP polo shirt that was part of the attendance gift package.

The Oracle rooftop Xmas parties were something else! The industry was certainly hot and buzzing then, and the mid November to late December calendar was always full of tech Xmas parties, where it was not unusual for more than one to be scheduled on the same evening. The Oracle rooftop event was one not to be missed. Quality food with quality drinks and Brisbane rooftop views. Hosted by Dave Redden (GM of Oracle Qld), a pleasant friendly fellow, who seemed to have a genuine interest in encouraging women into technology. He was proud of female numbers at Oracle, and each year used to give me a tour and updated me on progress.

APICTA held some very popular balls to honour award winners. These were always glam events of full ball gowns and tuxedos, where the mix of business, socialising and keeping the industry buzz alive mingled seamlessly.

A significant number of Queensland innovations and firms were promoted through these events. As with the regional tours, the media seemed keen and interested, and certainly ran a series of stories.

During these intense socialising times lots of business was not only discussed but also closed. Once, a multi-million dollar deal was closed while I and some industry colleagues were in the cable car chairlift ride from Kuranda down to the Cairns coastline.

These days people seem to be trying to recapture what we had back then. We operated in a no barriers, no borders, everyone-in-it-together approach, that aimed to increase the activity and productiveness and economy of the entire IT community, while enjoying the ride along the way. It resulted in growth and strong bonds as well as pride in our technology industry. An IT connection economy was alive and well decades ago.

Even though they consumed my time and energy, I miss those days.

***

Sonja's Tips: Networking is a lot of WORK, that you hope will NET you benefits at some future time. However, do not lose yourself in the networking chase: make sure you keep time to focus on your paid work as well.

Girls Do IT Too

A variety of WIT media. Bottom left hand is from the first Xmas party with Joan Sheldon in attendance.

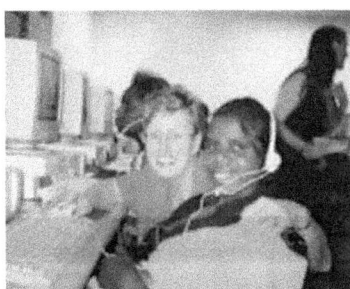

CH4 3 WIT also engaged in remote and rural communities. This is in Cairns with Dr Leslie Clarke, the member for Baron. I am standing in the background. We conducted tech awareness for local indigenous communities.

Packing swag bags for the first WIT Career Day. It was an enormous event. A full day that after we set up busloads of school kids pulled up at the front door and the day took off at full speed.

Girls Do IT Too

Paula, Kim, Maryse, Kim.

Dianne, Debbie, Julia, Sonja.

WIT 20th celebration Ann Uldridge and me.

Bernadette Hyland-Wood, me, Glenda Stone (nee Slingsy).

There are at least 3 past WiT Presidents in this. L to R- me, Barbara Tobin, 2 other people I do not personally recall and Anne-Marie Birkill.

Girls Do IT Too

Our wedding in 1999 I was almost 40 and Robin was 44.   Our Daughter born in 2003 A mother again at the age of 44.

CH4 9 The Courier Mail headline. Credit Story and Photo- Courier Mail.jpg

APICTA Gala Ball. L to R - me, The Honourable Terry Mackenroth, Mellissah Smith.

Another Year another APICTA Gala Ball. L-R- Margo and Peter Poole, The Honourable Terry Maackenroth, Myself and my Husband Robin Craig.

Years after APICTA in Qld folded I came across this old faded sign on a building in Milton, Brisbane. Ah memories...

2011- World's greatest Shave. Went from long to bald and raised a good sum of funds for the cause.

GOOD CAUSE:
ThoughtWare CEO Sonja Bernhardt.

The Courier Mail produced a cartoon of my involvement. I Love this cartoon it's rather accurate even the clothing is a suit I used to wear. I never met the artist, but they captured me perfectly – such talent!!

2019- John Grant and I at Qld iAwards, he was the honoured guest speaker, my company was recognised in 2 of the categories.

BuziWomenMedia 1.

BuziWomenBillboard.

BuziWomen Media3.

Girls Do IT Too

BRISBANE CIRCLE

Networking for Brisbane Women

October Edition Vol 13 No 3

What happened to the women's web?

We were promised a revolution, but all we got was horoscopes, diet tips and parenting advice.

Well, how about a new site - an intelligent site, a business site, an Australian site with global savvy?

It's here and it's all that.

Buziwomen.com. A revolutionary website for the intelligent woman, providing information on doing business and travelling, both overseas and to Australia. Buziwomen.com will cover cultural do's and don'ts, ethics, language tutorials, translation services and travel tips (for example where to stay and eat). More importantly, safety tips for women.

Well known Queensland businesswomen, Adrienne Ward (Chairman) and Sonja Bernhardt (Deputy Chairman) have wide and varied careers researching, assisting and mentoring women.

Adrienne, a former Telstra Businesswoman of the Year, says, "Buziwomen is an information based website for women who are travelling overseas for either business or pleasure.

The ability to log on anywhere in the world or to take a CD with them, will ease the anxieties many women face in unkown country".

A unique feature is the online video interviews with experienced business travellers giving advice, from how to present at the boardroom table in Japan to safety tips in New York.

With support from the Queensland Government and alliances globally, Buziwomen.com will also encourage women from other countries to come to Australia, not only to do business but also to enjoy what we have to offer.

Buziwomen.com will be coming to your screens and billboards very soon, so to register your interest, send an email to: sonja@buziwomen.com or call Adrienne on:

0417 499 384.

Buziwomen.com - Information for today's smart woman.

BuziWomen Adrienne Ward and I became the cover story on the Brisbane Circle magazine.

Girls Do IT Too

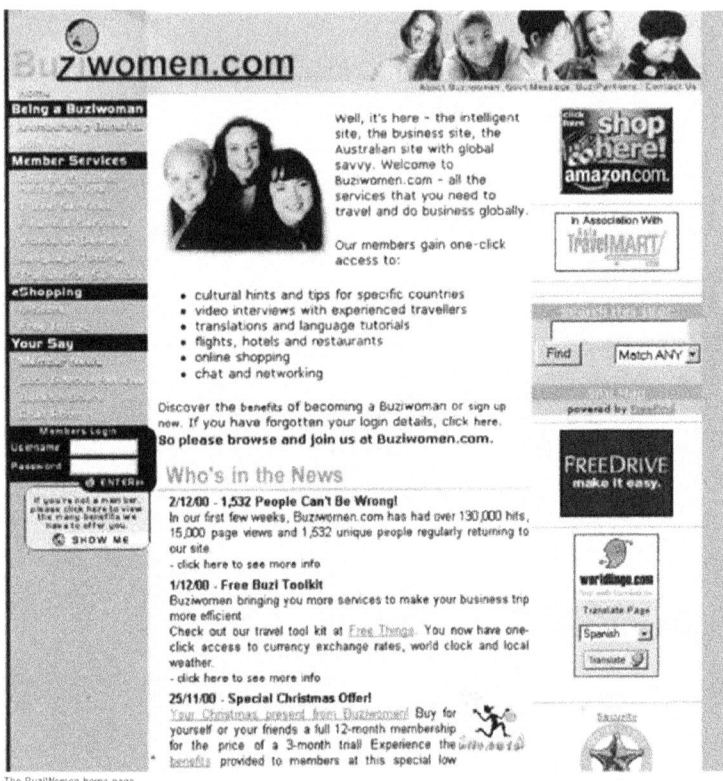

The BuziWomen home page.

6 The Award and Credibility Tango

Taking the Bar Higher

> *There is no point at which you can say, "Well I'm successful now. I might as well take a nap" —*
> *Carrie Fisher*

And the winner is….

Oft-provided advice is to build your credibility and profile, such as winning awards. This aims to gain greater trustworthiness and perceived reliability, leading to enhanced success. I'm not talking about subscribing to the "Fake It Until You Make It" concept (a saying that I was never fond of). Nor am I talking about getting more likes and followers on social media. Instead, I mean the old-fashioned style of winning personal credibility in your industry by entering and being recognised in awards, presenting at conferences, sitting on committees and being a sought-after expert commentator.

Oh, the anticipation and thrill when sitting on seats trying to look calm and together while waiting to hear the announcement and your name called. The silent words your mind is telling yourself while waiting to hear the result. "And the winner is" are words that send thrilling excitement through the winners and rapid disappointment and sometimes disbelief through those whose names are not called out.

A disappointing fact of business is that some people are automatically assigned greater credibility because of the *company* they work for, especially if it's a global brand name. In people's minds they tend to think that if you work for a large, respected company, you must be pretty great yourself. However, for a female small business owner, and especially in a non-traditional female field, the dance to gain credibility is a longer slog. It needs to be multi-faceted, spanning authorship, responsibility, commitments, community engagements and awards.

Committing to Committees

Blind Freddy could have predicted my future of committee involvement from my youth. Both of my parents had actively volunteered on a variety of committees (Rotary, Inner Wheel, Lions, Golf etc.). No doubt Dad would have taken a role on the local RSL club as well, if that had been allowed to a former German soldier and (albeit involuntary) Hitler Youth!

As early as primary school I committed to volunteer and leadership activities at school. In high school I was the School Captain. At the University of Queensland I became the social convenor for Union College, and even as a single parent years later doing my post graduate course, I voluntarily became the women's convenor for the QUT campus. So I should have seen my committee life coming: it was obviously in my genes. And after all I *was* the middle child, so perhaps it also had something to do with a way to gain attention.

I definitely "did my time" voluntarily serving on committees, boards, advisory panels, research grants and the like. I probably overdid it actually. When I look at the wide variety of local, state, national and some international bodies I became involved with, I sometimes wonder how I managed it. Wearing a cynical hat, I sometimes wonder whether it did do its supposed magic and add credibility to myself and my company.

Maybe, probably.

It's a bit like money spent on marketing: often you are never really sure if it made a difference, or if you would have had an uptake organically anyway. But it's something that you feel you need or are urged to do anyway.

I have come across an entire community of people who are professional committee and board members. They promote their credibility for and seek appointments on boards and committees, treating it as a career. As indeed it is, with income from paid positions. The unpaid positions are the credibility and experience stepping stones to paid ones. But for me it was about areas of interest and passion, and I never undertook committee commitments for remuneration, nor for the sole purpose of credibility. Many were committees for organisations I had created and built myself, born out of my own passion; some I was so delighted to be invited to join that saying no wasn't an option;

and others were award programs, where I was intensely interested in the added knowledge I acquired and the continued industry buzz from innovations and possibilities. Most appointments I served on actively and productively, though I admit there were a handful I barely contributed towards. Generally, if I felt I wasn't contributing or adding value I removed myself. That felt better than the guilt of being appointed but being non-productive.

"A committee takes hours to put into minutes what can be done in seconds": that quote from Judy Castrina is quite telling. I did always strive to be productive and for committees to streamline how they worked, but sometimes it felt that just getting in and doing without the committee process would achieve more.

Once, when I was on an international delegation as part of a committee, we had received invitations from the Australian trade commissioner to attend a cocktail party. All very exciting for me! Off I went, suitably attired and excited, to discover zero alcohol was being served. Stunning food, but absolutely no alcohol at all. I asked an aide, who reported that the commission was being respectful to the mostly Muslim country, so they weren't serving alcohol at the event. I continued to network and, while among a group of country's leaders, I made a joke about the difference of a cocktail party with no alcohol, and that perhaps it ought to be renamed to something more accurate.

There was an instant reaction.

The big boss man leant closer to me and said, "So, Sonja, you would like a drink, would you? What would you like?" and he reeled off a list of many varieties.

"Champagne would be fabulous!" I said.

He clicked his fingers and bingo, trays of alcoholic drinks started appearing. The group I was speaking with were the first to partake. Perhaps others were just waiting for someone else to express an interest, as they then could indulge as well. I was happy to be the trigger.

In 2005 I was an invited member of a federal advisory group, where we discussed and proposed approaches regarding the lack of participation of women in the technology sector. That culminated in a major summit, titled "partICipaTion summit" that was held in September 2005. The advisory panel meetings were always full of interesting people, discussions and ideas, and the summit was an invitation-only event for around 70 prominent leaders, drawn from the technology sector, educational intuitions and government, to consider the important issue of participation in ICT. I felt valued being in such a group and having my opinions matter.

The summit was held at The Westin in Sydney. With the exception of some magnificent hotels in Jakarta and my Manilla penthouse incident I had never stayed in such a grand hotel. I called my husband to tell him about how impressive it was. The excitement was building, and the next morning the event began with a rousing welcome by the famous Maxine McKew and the Minister (Senator the Hon. Helen Coonan), followed by an international keynote address. Unfortunately for me, I had rapidly started to become very unwell. I rushed to the bathroom and realised I was on a downward spiral of being *really* unwell. I went back to my hotel room, called the doctor after much vomiting, then passed out from a blinding headache and spent the rest of the day in Saint Vincent's hospital. The Minister even called in at the end of the day to see how I was going.

I flew home, still unwell, to be treated back on the Gold Coast for some issue that was causing pressure inside my nose. Goodbye Summit for me, as I missed all of the rest of it, as well as my luxurious hotel room.

Another time in 2008, when I was a member of the International Taskforce for Women and ICTs (a United Nations-supported committee) and also co-coordinator of the Asia Pacific Centre for Women and Technology (part of a global hub of 10 centres), I even received an invitation to attend the United Nations Division of Advancement of Women (DAW) at the United Nations Secretariat in New York. That was a big-ticket item.

An Awarding Time

I *love* judging award programs. Discovering the talent out there refreshes my faith in the future. My three all-time favourites have been the Asia Pacific IT Awards (APICTA), The Young ICT Explorers Awards (YICTE), and the Secrets of Australian IT Innovations (now defunct).

The Secrets of Australian IT Innovations launched as part of the 2002 World IT Congress. I was invited to be a judge and happily accepted the challenge. Off to Adelaide I trotted, not really knowing what to expect. It was so informative.

I saw Bill Clinton give his keynote talk, which included his ideas about the technical failures that lead up to the World Trade Centre disaster of 9/11. He spoke knowledgeably and managed question and answer time with expertise and aplomb. That speech gave me a small insight into the man post the Lewinsky controversy. I almost understood: he oozed a special something while on stage that could easily put you under his spell. Yes, even almost me, despite my own personal thoughts about him and the circumstances. At those awards I also met interesting people I remained in touch with over time, including the consummate Leila Henderson, the fascinating Sharon Don, and the adroit Matthew Michalewicz.

In 2006, Sharon agreed to become Ms March in my Screen Goddess IT Calendar, where she parodied the Ursula Andress white bikini beach scene from the James Bond Movie *Dr No*. That was one of the images that garnered significant media interest. Sharon looked stunning, and at the time was a telecommunications executive and a grandmother to boot.

Matthew Michalewicz ironically went on to publish the book *Winning Credibility: A guide for building a business from rags to riches*. I was honoured that Matthew invited me to be an early reviewer and commentator on that book.

I remained a judge on the Secrets innovation awards for a number of years. In 2004, I was thrilled to be invited to write the foreword for the "Secrets of Australian IT Innovation" web site. The foreword for the 2003 competition had been written by Bob Hayward (Vice President for Asia Pacific of the Gartner Group), so perhaps that invitation was a sign of my increasing credibility.

In 2001, I was amused to receive a call from the Australian Institute of Project Management. They ran annual Project Management awards, which previously had been for building and construction, but they had started receiving entrants from IT projects. The mystery of unknown technology must have seemed a little scary to them, so they felt they needed to get an IT person involved in the awards. My amusement came from my theory that project management was project management, regardless of the underlying aspects, but out of curiosity I accepted the invitation.

I remained involved from 2001 to 2006, in fact doing my usual and taking on board extra responsibility as the chief judge for Queensland in those awards. I judged both building and construction and technology projects, and was living proof that... yes, project management is project management, and the same principles and practices apply across sectors. Unfortunately, what I learnt about building and construction did not save me when I had renovations and extensions done to my own home – but that's a story for another time.

One thing I have learnt from both judging awards and being a nominee is that in the end it is a matter of practice and perfecting. The more awards you enter, the better you became at crafting award applications and learning to address the specific criteria – the better your elevator pitch becomes and the faster the process is for you, as you have previously prepared material to modify and tune with each application. Also, those who frequently enter awards may have a higher probability of being recognised simply because they have learnt and tuned the entry process. Each award does have a process that affects the weighting of the judging scale. That is one reason why awards are not necessarily true reflections of "the best of the best". The quality of your application may be more important than the quality of your product.

Once when I was two hours away from going on a holiday I noticed that a specific national award had opened for nominations. The close date was while I would be away on a cruise without internet access, so in a rush, but armed with prior award nomination material and evidence, I entered those awards. We became a national finalist. Given the entire application took me less than 30 minutes to pull together, that was amazing. Well really the credit goes to our pre-prepared material from past nominations.

By way of an example that awards may not reflect the best of the best, one strong memory from the APICTA awards was when I was part of the international judging panel for entries from across Asia and Australia. At a judging review session where judges' scores were displayed, it became obvious that one of the country's judges had not, how shall we say, objectively judged their own country's nominations. The skewing and comparison to the other judges' scores was stark. It wasn't an easy situation to manage and required diplomacy at very high levels. Luckily the judging chair was an ex-United Nations chairperson, and he stepped us through the situation and managed to maintain calm in the judging room.

It turned out that the country in question had told their judges that if they did not come back with a win, they faced severe penalties on their return. Rather drastic, inhumane and unfair really. Due to the potential international incident, we all ended up having to accept what had happened. One major lesson I learned as a direct result was that sometimes winning may be due to unknown political or other criteria, so never take it personally or too hard if you do not win. You never know what transpired behind the scenes. Better that you lose an award than someone loses their head.

You don't have to win to get benefits. I have observed that at times those who do not win can garner more publicity and media interest than the winner. A subtle change of the words to say Award Recognised, instead of Award Finalist, still allows for media releases, and inclusion of your award recognition in email signatures helps extend the message. It is more how you promote things than what you have. Those who win but who don't externally market or promote their win, and instead let the award gather dust, don't gain much public notice, do they?

One year the APICTA international award delegation was invited to dine at the Prime Minister of Malaysia's palatial private residence in Putrajaya near Cyberjaya. This was the beginning days of the Multimedia Super Corridor and Malaysia's Silicon Valley. We had toured Cyberjaya, it was incredibly impressive. The idea behind bringing together technology firms and workers' accommodation at Cyberjaya was brilliant, as was the idea of moving government administration to Putrajaya to avoid city traffic congestion. I note that subsequentially Cyberjaya suffered from multiple issues and has not yet become the success it has promised. However, Putrajaya kept growing in size and success.

As an evening activity, we attended the palace for a welcome reception and dinner. I was so full of expectations. The entrance area, dining room and toilets certainly lived up to my expectations of extreme grandeur. I had been looking forward to seeing how amazing a Malaysian dinner at the palace would be, sampling all the local flavours. Even thinking about it made my mouth water with anticipation. Much to my surprise and disappointment, the dinner menu was lobster bisque and USA beef. To the catering team it was an honour for them to serve such foreign and expensive specialties for the honoured foreign visitors. So, the food was delicious but was not the Malaysian Banquet I had expected. However, the entertainment was grand, and included the Prime Minister's favourite singer.

When it came to entering awards for myself and my company, I was restricted from a few, either because I was on the committee behind the awards, or I was a judge. Over time though, I personally, and my company, achieved a number of award recognitions, wins and finalists.

My favourite award acceptance speech was in 2014 when I accepted the IT in Aged Care (ITAC) ICT Company of the Year Award. The ceremony was in Hobart, Tasmania, land of my birth, so I was already on a high; plus two of our clients had been announced winners earlier in the evening for implementing our platform. My acceptance speech was fairly short, with the key message being that we listened to the sector to see what they needed: so I thanked the aged care industry for letting me "steal their IP" and put it into our software, thus making us award winning. The entire floor, including the MC, burst out laughing, as did I. But in fact, it was the truth, in that a key part of our success was learning from the needs and best practices of our clients.

Highest Achievements

Two personal award highs for me were being inducted into the International Women in Technology (WITI) Hall of Fame held in Silicon Valley in 2005, and being awarded a Medal of the Order of Australia (OAM) for my services to IT, on Australia Day in 2011.

To accept the WITI induction I, my husband (Robin) and young daughter (Kira) travelled to America, making it a part holiday as well. I also attended the WITI conference the day before and presented on one of the panels, where I met the famous US author and commentator, now ranked in the top 50 world thinkers (how's that for credibility), Nilofer Merchant. Years later, with her permission I quoted Nilofer and her research in my book *Women in IT in the New Social Era*.

Before arrival in Silicon Valley we had visited Disneyland, where my husband suddenly became very unwell and stayed in the motel room on our second day there. I had assumed he had "man flu" so was a little cross with him – he would say I was *very* cross with him.

We flew from Los Angeles to San Francisco, and took a rather bumpy ride in a minivan with very poor suspension to our Silicon Valley hotel, where Robin rested but remained unwell. He managed to put on a good front to make it to the WITI presentation evening. We departed for home the next day, when he was so obviously unwell that I wouldn't let him approach anyone at the airport counter in case we were banned from flying (and all this years before COVID-19). On arrival back home he went immediately to our doctor and was diagnosed with bacterial pneumonia and in desperate need of treatment. Boy did I feel bad, assuming he was being a wuss with man flu. My lesson there: man flu exists but sometimes they really are sick.

When Australia Day 2011 came around, my OAM news became official, but the actual investiture wasn't until 25 May. It was a day with a lovely blue sky but cool, and my mother (Olive), son (Tom), husband (Robin) and best friend (Lorraine) formed my supporting contingent. I recall the Queensland Governor, Penelope Wensley, suggesting I wear the small pin every day and talk about the honours program to raise awareness as more women ought to be nominated. At that time, I was the first female Queenslander to receive an OAM for services to IT, and only the fourth in Australia. I think it took another nine years for the second to be awarded. On the Queen's Birthday list in 2020, Jenine Beekhuyzen was awarded an OAM for services to IT. Jenine is another person who popped in and out of my life over the years, and I was happy to see that her work on intervention activities for girls in technology was recognised.

My personal sadness about me being awarded an OAM was that in November 2010 my dad was dying from Parkinson's-related complications, and a few days before his death I was sitting by his bedside. He wasn't really responsive or able to move. By that stage I had been confidentially advised that I was to be honoured with the award on Australia Day in 2011, but because of my honesty and strict compliance, stupidly didn't tell Dad about it. It is likely he would have heard, despite his unresponsiveness, and may have felt that sense of joy and pride that his daughter, the daughter of an immigrant, was being awarded such a high honour. I don't know if he would have heard it even if I had told him, but I still torture myself about this.

Once when being interviewed I was asked if there was anything I regretted, and my eyes filled with tears as I spoke about not letting my dad know, due to my insane sense of compliance. The interviewer (Frank Yarsley from Change Maker) kept it in the footage, as he felt there was a good lesson there for people taking things as too black and white. And he's right.

I spent Christmas 2010 and New Year 2011 with my husband and daughter, on what became our induction to a great passionate pastime. We went on our first cruise. This one was in the Mediterranean, a dream holiday with Christmas in Venice then boarding the cruise and visiting Bari in Italy, Rhodes in Greece, Alexandria in Egypt where we did a full day's trip to the Pyramids, Katakolon in Greece where we visited the site of the original Olympics, Dubrovnik in Croatia where we were amazed at the city wall, then back to Venice. At the end of the cruise, on debarkation I found an expensive looking diamond ring in the ladies' toilet. I handed it in to the customer services desk, and when they thanked me for my honesty, I shot back, "Yep, that's me, honest," thinking of my failure to tell my dad; so in a stab at myself I added, "When I get back to Australia they are going to award me."

Another prestigious honour I have received was in November 2019, when I was elevated to the Pearcey Hall of Fame for distinguished lifetime achievement and contribution to the development and growth of Australian Technology. The ceremony was in Melbourne, and again my mother, husband and daughter Kira attended. My mother was in high demand that night, the young people wanted to talk to her as she is witty and wise, and the older widowed gentlemen were rather taken with her. It was a very enjoyable evening, topped off with this additional honour added to my belt.

The list goes on.

The Third Degree

And of course, at the other end of my career I had my university qualifications. After dropping out of university in the 1970s, I went on to complete my studies, although not in science; I was awarded a Bachelor of Arts (Maths and Psychology) in 1987, a post graduate degree in Business Administration (Human Resource Management) in 1989, and a Masters of Business Administration in 1992.

If that's not enough credentials and honours to gain credibility, then there *is* something wrong.

There is a funny story about my acceptance to undertake my MBA. I was working at Mincom at the time and received a scholarship-like offer to do an MBA. I had never applied for it, it just arrived in the mail, maybe they were trying to increase the female intake at that time. I marked the offer off as a non-acceptance, as I was dedicated and loyal to my work, and loving it. I put the response into its envelope and placed it at the reception area for the post.

A short while later I was chatting with Jane Reid and told Jane what I had done. She was *furious* with me. Telling me what an *idiot* I was, and that I should have accepted the study offer. She grabbed my hand and marched me out to the reception area, where the mail had not yet been sent and took back my letter, forcing me to change it to acceptance. And so, I ended up going back to university. And a few years later I was rehired by Mincom at twice my salary – so if I never thanked you Jane – thanks.

When I was doing my MBA, I was a single parent of two young children and I completed this two-year qualification in one year plus summer school, holding down a job in the technology sector simultaneously. I managed early completion by doing more than the recommended subjects per semester and doing two subjects at summer school. I'm pretty sure that's where I finely tuned my project management skills and an efficient and effective way of doing things.

We had a colour coded calendar on the home fridge. It was a guide for me and my children about time blocks and what activities to do when. I had to schedule in blocks of "do not disturb Mum", and blocks of "make Mum stop studying to spend time with you." It worked brilliantly for all of us.

Spreading the Word

But wait, there's more.

I set up mentoring programs and have also been a mentor through a range of programs. For example I spent five years with APESMA (The Association of Professional Engineers, Scientists and Managers Australia), where I was delighted to mentor people from a wide range of disciplines, including an equine vet (Dr Jennifer Stewart) who has gone on to reach fame in her field, and a technician at the early stages of his career who became a cloud architect (Scott Carpenter). I also spread the technology and women in technology word in the media. I spent more than a decade as the resident "geek girl" on ABC radio, covering a variety of technology topics of interest to the general public. Many topics of which I then updated and turned into cruise ship talks. I crafted numerous articles for traditional publications, and also authored three books for an international publishing house, and contributed chapters to two other books.

I have been a presenter including keynote at business conferences. I did many, many presentations at schools, and once even had a busload of Brisbane school senior students turn up at my house to gain some hands on, real world "life in a technology company" experience.

It was certainly different for them, as most expected a corporate company but found themselves in a residential area, where the road was so skinny the bus could not turn around and had to go further up to a roundabout and then park on my front lawn. Not quite the same as sweeping up to some grand foyer. The kids tumbled out of the bus and into my house, where we had set up three different areas, and they split into groups. In one area they were taught to pull apart a server and see the workings inside it. In another they listened to a consultant and data analyst and saw the type of work they did. The third area was with me where I talked about owning a technology business, and marketing approaches. From the feedback received the day was considered highly successful.

I also did my rounds of technology presentations at Rotary, Lions and Zonta clubs. I also travelled up the eastern coast of Queensland speaking to community and educational groups. With presentations as diverse as speaking with groups of Aboriginal and Torres Strait Islander year 10 and year 11 students in Far North Queensland, to city-based talks with professional men and women on the impact of changes in science and technology, to presentations at school career days. I've been listed in multiple Who's Who publications, including the 2008, one time only published "Who's Who in Tasmania", which I found rib tickling. When I was advised I was being included I said, "Umm, well I live in Queensland and am in the Queensland Who's Who and the national Who's Who of Australian Women, so I'm not sure if I qualify for the Tasmanian one." The response was a resounding "Yes you do: you were born in Tasmania and that qualifies you!"

Measuring Success

The credibility, recognition and award tango can lead to great opportunities for team sharing and celebrations. Award nominees often mention that even just crafting their application helped the company reflect on their successes. Naturally, sharing news companywide can help spark togetherness, be it about a keynote talk, award entry, mention in the media and so on. At many award events we would take out a table or part table and have clients and staff mixed together enjoying the event (pre-COVID of course!). I even generously went to the extent of offering to clients who entered and were finalists, that I would fund their attendance at the award event, and some of our staff would accompany them. To me, seeing our product through the eyes of our clients was a great success measure, and I felt the added motivation that paid travel to the award ceremony encouraged entrants, which helped publicise our product.

Despite all of that, I do feel it's important that you do not measure your success by the perceptions of others. What matters is what is important to you. The classic career rise to the top may not be the success measure for you; acceptance and respect of your peers may not be you success measure; designer clothes may not be your success measure. I suggest taking time out to consider what success means for you, and to then follow that path. For me it's what makes me happy and inspired.

The credibility tango can be exhausting.

I have to admit that when living it I enjoyed it immensely, but it did take up a lot of my time, energy and money. In retrospect, I'd suggest it's not really necessary to do as much as I did when I jumped into, or perhaps fell into, the credibility dance. You might find that you end up with a lot of credibility among people in the wrong places to be your clients. However, if you feel your career or company needs a boost, some credibility may be a bonus to assist you on your way to achieving your personal and business goals.

When I stop and analyse my personal involvements it's obvious that many were above and beyond suggested career credibility activities, and that my own passion drove me to take more on board. Ultimately, the vast majority were more about following my own interests and inspirations.

Once in a possible Tall Poppy Syndrome moment, I overheard an Office for Women representative describe me as an over-achiever. At the time I ironically wondered if that comment would have been made if I was male or if I would have been labelled instead an ambitious achiever. For years I kind of ignored that comment but in truth it semi upset me a little. Looking back I'm inclined to think that the commenter was on the right track. She is likely to be right. Don't try to be that over achiever. Try not to set rigid almost impossible levels to achieve.

I recall a respected colleague told me once that she'd lowered her usual standard of work effort and no one had noticed. It was a self-driven standard that she had set and measured herself on, but to others, even at a lower standard her work was still exemplary. Interesting lesson there.

Maybe I needed to learn to say, "No"? I know I should have learnt to say, "Sure I'm interested, and the rate to engage me to do it is $x".

***

Sonja's Tip: Lessons from the Tango are: Find your balance. Be completely in the moment and if you are going to Tango do it with intent.

7 Sonja in Wonderland

Distractions in the Wider World

I almost wish I hadn't gone down that rabbit hole – and yet – and yet – it's rather curious, you know. This sort of life! – Alice

---

There are not only business rabbit holes one might chase or fall into, but personal ones that can cause major disruptions and distractions. Along the road to growing and selling my software business I took side trips down both, not only failed business ideas but health concerns and some major personal passions. I was a bit like Alice exploring a new world and being amazed at the wonder of it all, even if sometimes I was lost. I was missing my own Cheshire Cat for directions.

There were a few Mad Hatters, however.

Some people have a single-minded drive, willing to leave all else in a distant second place to their business ambitions. But for most of us, in the end life is a delicate juggle of family, work, health and personal passion projects. I admit I tipped too heavily into the passion areas. That meant my energy, time and sometimes money were all consumed, while the business suffered through delayed growth and lack of careful attention. I undertook female technology intervention projects and academic book writing that became all consuming, at what I believe was the cost of business growth.

Witty Passions

As a woman in IT, I could not help but notice how many men were in the field. Sometimes the whole industry looked like a sea of men in suits. But there was me, and I knew others. What could be done to address this disparity?

"Attraction, Promotion, and Retention" has been my catch-cry and that of many passionate activists in this field around the globe for almost four decades. Yet to date the secrets of attracting females to study technology, enter technology careers and stay in technology industries, and of how best to navigate promotional pathways, have not been found. More accurately, many ideas have been found, tested and failed. But that does not stop people from trying and trying again. It certainly did not stop me.

In addition to my Women in Technology activities, I co-created the national umbrella group AWISE (Australian Women in IT and Science Entity, the last part later renamed to Science and Engineering). Beyond Australia I co-created, with Dr Patrice Braun, the Asia Pacific Centre for Woman in Technology (APCWIT); and I eagerly undertook a range of individual projects and academic writing on the subject.

Not only did I undertake personal projects, I applied my passion inwards to my own business. My technology company had at least 85% female representation, and for most of the time 100% of coders were female, so I wasn't just hiring females into the "soft roles" of marketing and office administration. My business analysts, data scientists, coders and project managers were female, as a deliberate strategy.

From 2017, the catch cry of "You cannot be what you cannot see" and the interchangeable "If you can see her you can be her" was increasing in popularity. Personally, I don't subscribe to that piece of current wisdom, even though my life's passion included lots of role modelling, career days and presentations. To me I interpret the "cannot be" and "see her" wisdom as limiting your options to dream and imagine and create your own path and role. I prefer a catch cry that is more about being, "Curious, Creative and Clever and designing your own future" to one that basically says see what's around and copy that.

IT Goddesses

All of my individual projects were immense fun to work on. The *Screen Goddess IT Calendar* (www.itgoddess.info) in 2006 is my personal favourite, despite costing me $25,000 of personal funds and despite the backlash I received: there was even a Denial of Service (DoS) attack on the server by people who disagreed with the approach.

Screen Goddess was labelled controversial by the media as it supposedly featured naked women. It actually did not, it was entirely discreetly done. It was a parody of iconic movie scenes, each month featuring a real woman who was working in IT, with most months also featuring technology objects, sometimes hidden or as part of a puzzle, as part of the overall image. However, media spread the negative view. Some people said I had conned all the women involved into participating. What power I had and didn't know. Some people said if I had used models instead of real women in real technology careers that would have been received better. I still dispute that, as the entire idea was to show that there are real women in technology and they are multi-dimensional with a fun, witty side.

One of my respected industry contacts, John Grant, asked me not to communicate with him about the topic. That actually upset me. In 2016 John was involved in his own significant media controversy when he was chairman of the Australian Rugby League Commission, and I'm sure he saw first-hand the many misleading things that can be spread by the media. It really can be a circus.

I sometimes wonder if the calendar had featured men the response would have been different. In fact, I'm sure it would have been: hypocrisy in attitudes to men and women is to this day still widespread.

The coverage and interest in Screen Goddess spread globally. I vividly recall a phone call in the middle of the night from the BBC for an unscheduled interview. In an amusing twist I even received messages from a Sonya Bernhardt from America, who had authored the book *Texas – Land of the Big Hair: Big Money Divorce Texas Style*. When CNN was interviewing her, to her surprise they showed my profile, not hers! She apparently just sat there and watched the profile, a little stunned, but did not report the discrepancy comment to them as it was Live TV. There were some minor coincidental links: like mine, her husband was in technology, and she had a link to Australia. But that was it – her name is even spelt differently to mine. What can I say… lazy journalist?

The American Sonya contacted me to thank me for being a decent person who had an interesting life and for being her "stand up" character. Another Sonja Bernhardt, this time from Germany, also contacted me to thank me for the sudden fame she was enjoying in her hometown. It is interesting that when Screen Goddess first hit the media, the biggest hits on the website came from Germany. I still don't know why.

I was secretly hoping that Oprah Winfrey or Ellen DeGeneres would contact me so that I could set the record straight and demonstrate how empowering the calendar actually was, and for it to be celebrated. I did send them media releases, but alas it didn't happen.

The Screen Goddess calendar worked to unite the passionate volunteers involved and helped to bond people in a united cause. Many of those friendships remain today. I even had an original theme song written and sung for it. I'm still proud of that song and the message it delivers, it was written and sung[viii] by Alastair Lee Guinlee (© 2006):

Be a goddess or a queen, on that little screen,
Soar as high as you can go,
And be the star of your own show
Have the freedom to achieve,
And live what you believe
Release your mind and dream…yeah!

Reshape your world
Reshape your world….

However, while the calendar generated interest and encouraged some individuals, as far as I am aware it did not "work" in terms of attracting statistically more women into technology studies and careers. Though even years later I would receive requests from teachers for copies.

At the height of the media frenzy in late 2006, I was booked to present at a "Computers in Education" conference in Cairns. One of the conference sponsors tried to pressure the organisers into removing me because of the Screen Goddess calendar controversy, even though I wasn't talking about the calendar, going so far as threatening to withdraw their sponsor funds. The media turned up, did some interviews, took a super photo of me that I still have today, and ran the story. To their credit, the organisers stuck with me, and the next day my presentation was a full house with standing room only. There I was, a single person doing something I thought was of assistance, and a national powerful industry national association was afraid of me and wanted to shut me up. Maybe that was a good thing. It meant I was making a splash and a noise. A Brisbane City mayoral candidate once told me that it was when people started to lodge complaints or resist and media wrote up the controversy, that she knew she was starting to be listened to and was making a difference. There is wisdom in that comment.

We live in a peculiar world, where glamour is popular, "sex sells" and we are told to have a work-life balance. Yet show that women in IT can do all that, and you get in trouble.

Well I did.

Outside of the naysayers the calendar did garner some very positive feedback, like this comment from a professor at a leading Australian University:

We need multiple measures to attract people with different demographics. A great example of this is the "Screen Goddess IT Calendar." I should mention that while this initiative has triggered some negative reactions in certain sectors, it has generated more media interest and discussion of the ICT sector than a generation of well meaning pamphlets from the industry and industry associations. The controversy is an opportunity, it gives us a platform. The calendar also shows an alternative view of people in the ICT area in a brilliant way. We have a lot to offer very different people. We need to emphasise and exploit that diversity to generate interest.

Another anonymous correspondent said on the non-traditional initiatives:
Well done for raising public awareness to the extent that respected Business Journals are researching the declining participation of Australian women in the most lucrative technology roles, which underpin most modern business sectors. Raising public awareness outside industry circles is a difficult task for which you should all be congratulated.

Despite all that controversy and the extreme repair work required after the Denial of Service attack, I loved Screen Goddess. It was so much fun working on that project, and I'm proud of the outcome. I drew up a score card of what it achieved. Web site totals over a seven week period were in excess of 21 million hits, 2.3 million page views and 531,000 sessions. For over a week the story was the number one viewed story on both *The Age* and *Sydney Morning Herald*. The SMH mash up blog and the news.com.au blog were long running and attracted hundreds of comments/active participants.

Greater than 60% of sales were to females. 20% sales were overseas into 23 countries other than Australia: Ireland, Scotland, England, Germany, Austria, Switzerland, Hungary, Czech Republic, Netherlands, Norway, Sweden, Finland, Denmark, Italy, Portugal, France, Brazil, Argentina, Canada, USA, Singapore, Fiji, New Zealand. Hundreds of web blogs and forums sprang up. Stories ran in countries around the world. Magazines representing the target market of young women, ran articles or made mention of the calendar, e.g. *New Woman* in Australia and *For You* magazine in Germany. Dozens of radio interviews were held, mostly on the ABC radio network, which extended the reach into a number of regional and rural areas.

And it ticked the diversity criterion, with the models including African, Asian, Sri Lankan, European, Finnish, and white Australian ethnicities. Ages ranged from early twenties through to sixties. Roles ranged from database administration, programming & networking through to project management, sales, education, executive management and entrepreneurs. Diversity of movies selected included Hollywood, Bollywood and Disney movies.

In some ways I think if it was done today it would be celebrated as a shining light of female expression and ingenuity. I've been itching to do more since but never have, yet.

As a side note, the photographer, Jane Long, went on to win a number of photographic competitions and achieve some worldwide fame for her other work. Jane confessed that she'd always wanted to dress up in a Star Wars theme, so even though she wasn't technically in IT, she starred as Ms August,

Princess Leia in the slave scene.

Around the World

My second favourite passion project is the 2008 "Doing IT Around the World" Project (www.passionit.info). There I profiled 36 technology and science role model women across 24 countries around the world, even including Antarctica, and put together a diary of a day of their lives – all the same day – 11 August – their work, their lives, plus a pictorial profile and interview with each.

11 August was chosen as that was the day when the spread spectrum patent was awarded jointly to Hedy Lamarr and George Antheil. Given that Hedy Lamarr is more famous as a glamorous actress than a thinker, yet spread spectrum frequency hopping is the basis of what is used for mobile communications even today, I felt the day entirely suitable. That was one long day for me, 44 hours spanning the globe chasing the sun from sunrise in Antarctica to sunset in Hawaii. The usual expected UK, USA, Asia, Europe and Oceania were included, along with Scandinavia, Africa, Caribbean and the Mediterranean, so it was truly a global representation. The albums and diary are available for free download and were also converted into a course on Wikiversity. If I was doing this project again, I would improve the graphics and presentation of the diary and profiles, however the content is incredibly powerful and fascinating as it stands.

I had the idea of "Doing IT" when in May 2008 I was speaking at a conference in Arequipa, Peru, surrounded by women from around the world. I had been invited to speak at the combined Asia Pacific Economic Cooperation (APEC) and Latin America and the Caribbean (LAC) Digital Forum for Women event. In 2007 I had spoken at an APEC Advancing Women in the Digital Economy conference in Port Douglas, Queensland, and had made some key friendships, in particular Andrina Lever, who headed the International Women's Leaders Network and was deeply entrenched into APEC, and Patrice Braun, who knew how to navigate the APEC culture. So, either my speaking was very well received at the Port Douglas conference or one or both of these new contacts recommended me for the next year's meeting in Peru.

Whichever way it happened, it was of course incredibly exciting to be asked to present at such a venue. I did it in my usual style with lots of excited talking and hand movements: I only hope the many United Nations translators were able to follow what I had to say. The entire Peru trip was fascinating for me, and six incidents occurred that remain strong memories.

In one incident, Patrice Braun invited me into some meetings with the Peruvian delegates. The Forum was to be held at a brand-new convention centre, Cerro Juli. The centre was so new it was still a construction site. Patrice very diplomatically raised our concerns about this with the Peruvian delegate as the forum was to begin in two days' time.

The delegate was unfazed "Don't worry, we'll hire more people."

With our Australian sensibilities Patrice and I remained concerned as to how it would happen at all.

To our great surprise it all worked. Thousands of people were hired and worked solidly 24 hours a day for those two days and nights, so that on the day of the opening, which the president of Peru attended, the place was complete, sparkling and amazing. I was in awe. My awe faded a bit when after the first day the plumbing began to fail and doors started falling off, but it was sure sparkling and fabulous for the main media event at the launch.

Speaking of media events, I loved the conference, the environment and the food, especially the ceviche, which I had never eaten before. The Peruvian media noted my glowing enthusiasm, so they interviewed me as an example of how much foreigners loved their country. Years later someone told me they saw that TV show at the time and that my joy was obvious.

Another occurred on my first night in Peru when I went for a wander into the town. The power suddenly went off, and a couple of purse snatchers took advantage of the blackout to run up the street grabbing what they could. One tried for mine, but I hugged it close to my chest and was knocked aside with nothing stolen. I was a little rattled but quickly forgot about it, as on subsequent trips around town there were no incidents at all, and everything went extremely smoothly. Super-fast free broadband was available, so I could easily keep in touch with home, and I told my husband how fascinating and safe Peru was and suggested that we visit for a holiday. He kindly reminded me about the bag snatches on my first night and how after that all my travel was on a United Nations organised bus with UN provided security personnel. Perhaps it wasn't as safe as I now felt.

As I was from the Gold Coast, living at sea level, I experienced altitude sickness in Arequipa where the elevation is over two kilometres. The pain in the back of my head, not being able to face breakfast, and the vomiting were not pleasant. The friendly locals gave me the local cure which was a leaf tea. The bus driver also stopped and showed me where to buy some "cure" lollies, which were like barley sugar but with a liquid inside. They both worked.

In fact, they worked so well that at the key evening celebration event of the conference, everyone had so much energy that we danced and had fun all night long. A number of experienced conference attendees remarked how wonderful the country was, and how they'd never seen attendees with so much energy at night.

I thought they'd said that the "cure" was cocoa leaves, and I innocently told my husband that I never knew chocolate could fix altitude sickness, and asked him what could there be in cocoa leaves that would be so effective. His laconic reply: "I think you'll find that's coc*a*, not coc*oa*."

Oops.

It was my first, and only, dance with cocaine, and it was legal.

It was certainly the subject of discussion on the tour bus the next day when UN representatives raised the need to place a ban on the local substances. Apparently Peru's insistence on retaining their traditional cures has been a sore point with the UN.

One event that puzzled me was that apparently, in my usual Australian loud and to the point style, I had managed to say something that slightly offended the Korean delegation. After my talk they were keen to talk to me and discuss something, but I never found out what that was. When I spoke with the person charged with discussing the issue with me, I said something that made them change their minds. To this day I still don't know what the original issue was. But it still sometimes plays on my mind.

My sixth interesting experience from this trip to Peru was coming back into Australia. For the first time ever, I had ticked every box on the customs declaration. I had food, I had visited freshwater rivers, I had biological specimens, wood items, rocks and so on.

The customs officer looked at me and said, "You marked all of these as Yes."

I said, "That's because I did them all."

The officer verbally patted me on the back, "Ah, at least you are honest! Off you go!"

"But… but… I have butterflies!"

The officer looked at me and said "Oh, you have butterflies. Okay, come over here then." I was searched properly then and customs almost took the beautiful Amazonian butterflies off me, but luckily they managed to pass the test and I was allowed to keep them, as well as a wooden gourd gift from the conference, which ironically, was taken off another attendee.

My husband's response to this story was a blunt, "You idiot." We still joke about, "But I have butterflies!"

I started *Doing IT* almost the day I got home from Peru and rapidly completed the project, launching it in September 2008.

Another passion project I undertook in 2008 was the "IT's Million $ Babes Awards", which were about recognising women in IT who run million-dollar technology businesses. They are the creators and innovators who have achieved financial success and are living their life dreams and helping transform the lives of others.

The awards were only presented twice. There were six inaugural winners. Among them was Liesl Capper, CEO of My Cyber Twin. Liesl went on to sell her Artificial Intelligence engine to IBM as a foundational component of IBM Watson. Five winners comprised the second award presentation. By then the world was suffering from the impacts of the Global Financial Crisis, so I put an end to the awards, not because of a lack of women with million and multimillion-dollar companies, but due to the global sentiment at that time, it did not seem appropriate. I have never restored them.

To me the tricky thing about restoring these awards is that companies with significant investor funds are valued according to that. I'm a bit of a snob and prefer to value them on revenue or actual sale price, not unrealised future hopes. Most "tech unicorns" nowadays tend to fit the investor-valuation model. And perhaps this isn't the right time, with our sad contemporary backlash against the "rich and entitled". Still, I remain inclined to think that showing women can set up, run and own financially successful technology companies demonstrates great role models and gives young women something to aim for.

These high-profile industry projects resulted in comments and feedback from industry leaders and educationalists. They produced web-based discussions engaging not only those in the technology industries but the wider network that needed to be reached, e.g., parents, peers and teachers. All this before widespread social media.

In many ways I genuinely believe that my women in technology projects were ahead of their time, and certainly can be seen as pioneering ventures that helped lay the pathway for the many that followed.

I have a strong opinion about the whole work-life balance idea. I think it's basically a lie, setting people up for failure as it's impossible to find an equal balance. I don't even call it balance as to me that indicates if one side is up the other is down. Establishing a concept as work-life balance instantly means women will feel guilty when one aspect of their life is "down" even if another is "up". Instead I prefer to call it a "Portfolio" – it is a portfolio of my life and all the things I do that contribute to me as a whole person.

If I am spending more time with family or on volunteer passion activities that adds value and wisdom to me as a person, that enhances me and the way I operate in other parts of my portfolio, and vice versa. It's about the whole picture of me as a person and not opposite or opposing sides of my life.

Do I feel I might have invested too much of my time and myself in these projects? Yes. Do I regret doing them? No.

Authorship

While I had been writing articles for print magazines for a while, I almost accidentally became a traditionally published author with the publication of my first full book, *Women in IT in the New Social Era*[ix].

What happened was this. I was actively involved with my daughter Kira's primary school, a fledging Montessori school, and had undertaken the role as President of the Parents and Friends association. With a group of fabulous, enthusiastic parents (hello Cara, Jodi, Cassie, Julia and others), we had implemented a series of activities such as sushi deliveries on Fridays, weekly banking for the kids, and Mother's Day and Father's Day gift stalls. We were even successful in applying for funding to build and stock a library and install water fountains in the school.

One of the fabulous parents there was Candice Lemon-Scott, who is now gaining fame via her *Jake in Space* and *Eco-Ranger* young adult novels. In 2012 at one of the P&F events to help promote cross-business networking with the parents, I was MC for the event. As I listened to Candice talk about her writing, I asked her in question time if she could ghost write. She said yes, and we arranged for her to come and chat further. My idea was that she could ghost write my story about women in technology. I was too busy to write it myself, but happy to talk and pay someone else to write. She had another idea: she thought that the things I had to say ought to be written in an academic book. She went away, applied on my behalf to a publisher (IGI Global), and WOW: within a week or two I received an email offering to publish my book. A real publisher with a genuine offer.

I was impressed, much to the pain of my husband, who had written a number of intriguing science fiction novels yet none had been taken on by a traditional publisher. Here I was, not one word written, just a general concept, and an offer was on the table within a fortnight. Here he was, with completed and interesting novels waiting to be snapped up, but not a publisher in sight.

I accepted the offer and then… panicked.

How was I going to fit in growing my company, my home life, my volunteer activities and writing a book? And not just any book, but an academic text with a set timeline, specified formatting and full referencing; requiring ten to fifteen chapters of 10,000 to 14,000 words per chapter. That's between 100,000 to 210,000 words. Yes Mum, I know I talk a lot but…

Luckily, I discovered research assistant Valerie to help amass references, coffee and middle of night and early morning writing sessions. Coffee played such an important role I formally acknowledged it in my final book via this comment: "I must thank a piece of technology, my Nespresso™ coffee maker. Seriously – I wasn't much of a coffee drinker before, but I needed additional hours in the day to be able to manage my company during a growth phase, my home life and 'the book'. I enjoyed being a science experiment and proving that coffee really does stimulate you."

I took the unusual step of having two forewords in the publication. I invited two women I deeply respected to write them. Dale Spender, a widely published, high profile feminist, and a young Pia Waugh (now Andrews). Pia went on to become well known in Australia for her Government "open data ninja" activities. I first met Pia in 2006 at a women in technology career event in Western Australia, and was instantly impressed. I was delighted she accepted the invitation to write one of the forewords.

Having a formally published book is meant to add to or enhance your credibility. I'm not so sure, though maybe the issue with me was it being academic, rather than a novel, self-help or popular book. It sold a substantial amount of copies, and became part of seven selected series of books, plus had a video series created to further extend its message. But I don't think my own profile gained much from it.

As an academic book it was expensive, and likely to be read mainly by… academics. My chief messages from the book didn't and still don't fit the popular narrative of why there are relatively few women in technology, which amounts to our being victims of external factors. I went out on a limb and presented, backed up by research, an unpopular viewpoint that it is now mainly individual choice if girls enter technology or not.

Luckily, I'm not afraid to be unpopular nor to speak out.

That unpopular message was beautifully and succinctly expressed by my then ten-year-old daughter when I asked her that central question: "Why do you think some girls don't like computers?"

Her instant reply: "It's just how they are"… and in that lay the conclusion to my first book.

I went on to be the major contributor to another book (an updated version of my first book) and a minor contributor to another academic book on Blockchain. Now I have three books where I am the named author, plus two where I contributed an authored chapter.

Oh, and now this memoir.

Health Scares

In addition to my personal projects, I have survived personal health scares: being hospitalised with meningococcal meningitis (1996), cancer scare with fine needle biopsy for breast lumps (late 90s), and a life threatening, rapidly growing "benign" tumour (pleomorphic adenoma) in my mouth (2003). The tumour discovery and removal were all very rapid.

I was at the dentist when suddenly his voice changed, and I knew something was wrong. He was trying to sound light-hearted when he said, "Ah, Sonja. Have you recently burnt the top of your mouth?"

"No. Not that I'm aware of."

Next thing I knew I was at the specialist, who scheduled me for an operation a few days later. I had my dentist to thank for saving my life. Thanks Mark! It turned out that if the tumour had not been removed it would have grown up into my brain and affected speech, ability to swallow, and eventually even my ability to breathe. It was successfully removed just before Christmas in 2003.

One of my company staff representatives at that time was Jenine Beekhuyzen. Jenine came to work with me after I had presented at a conference panel and she approached me, giving me her CV on a small disc. I was impressed with her innovative approach and enthusiasm, so hired her. Jenine very kindly created speech cards for me for after the operation. It was so thoughtful and a smart, well researched practical gift. As it turned out I didn't need the cards, as apart from having a giant hole in roof of my mouth for months as it healed, I was able to speak fine. My mum was pleased.

In 2008 I was diagnosed with osteopenia and severe osteoarthritis in my hands, which is ironically due to occupational computer usage. What triggered me to get tested for the osteo was something that to this day I still find amusing. One of the fingers on my right hand started hurting; there was nothing evident, it just hurt. It kept hurting.

Feeling like a fool I went to my doctor and said, "my finger hurts". However, that statement triggered the testing which revealed both my osteopenia and the start of osteoarthritis. The arthritis is today more advanced, and my fingers have the classic wonky misshapen look. From time to time the pain reappears, and naturally some activities are now beyond the strength and grip of my hands; but mostly they are just what they are. I tried all the recommended treatments to no avail, so I just let them be. At one stage the doctor asked if I'd tried fish oil or arthritis tablets? I told him I had but they hadn't done anything.

The doctor said, "You may as well stop then, because they work for some people and not others."

Once I tried a new experimental cream, and it seemed to work. Then I realised what was actually working was the rubbing my hands regularly, not the specific cream. Beware the snake oils.

***

Sonja's Tips: Sarah Bernhardt, not my sister Sarah Bernhardt but the French actress (1844-1923), said: "Life begets life. Energy creates energy. It is by spending oneself that one becomes rich."

I did become experience and soul rich, but I expand the tip with this: Passion drives, passion burns, it creates its own wonderland; enter with your eyes open and beware of the depth of those rabbit holes and the cost to your core business.

Girls Do IT Too

I was a busy girl around town. This picture is one my favourites, wish I had the original. Credit for photo Leah Broadfoot and story is Brisbane News published in 2000.

2010- I made it to be cover girl (again). This is the APESMA magazine and that's me and my mentee of that year Scott Carpenter. Photo Credit- APESMA.

WIT Awards 2009 was 20's themed. Robin and I suitably attired. One of our staff members Natasha Hurst was an ex hairdresser and she coiffed my hair into 1920's perfection.

I won the ICT Outstanding Achievement Award.

2016- Here we (Michelle and I) are. Looks glamorous and a winning photo – right_. We are finalist here not winners but goes to show what message a red carpet and a glamour event can say.

Girls Do IT Too

2015- this was a win, well a win in our category for that month. Knowledge Management and IT Award. (Robin, Sonja and Tiffany).

2014- Winner ICT Company of the Year @ Aged Care IT Awards. My acceptance speech provoked much merriment. On stage from L to R- the MC Arron Wood, Me, Tiffany, Kim and Robin I love this photo.

ABC Radio resident. With Trevor Jackson.

MC'ing a WIT Panel.

Panel presentation WITI.

Blockchain talk where I re met Jane.

News of my 2005 induction into WIT Hall of Fame breaks.   Credit- Photo self-owned. Story- The Australian.

Robin and I at the WIT Hall of Fame Ceremony in Silicon Valley. He was struggling to be there as he had pneumonia at the time. I thought he had Man Flu.

With WITI Founder Carolyn Leighton, and the giant heavy award that was part of my induction into the Hall of Fame.

Girls Do IT Too

2011 News of being awarded an OAM broke Credit- Story-Business Acumen.

2011- Me grinning like a Cheshire cat waiting for my name to be called and OAM presented.

The Honourable Penelope Wensley AC – Queensland Governor presenting me with the Medal of the Order of Australia.

My Medal of the Order of Australia (OAM) support crew- L to R Tom (son), Robin (husband) me, Olive (mum), Lorraine (BFF).

2019- Elevation to the Pearcey Hall of Fame L to R- Nigel Warren (CSIRO - sponsor), me, Wayne Fitszimmons (Pearcey).

Screen Goddess Xmas photo for some special edition calendars.

The Screen Goddess launch at Movie World. L to R - The Honourable Chris Cummins, Sonja Bernhardt, Robin Craig – with rent a crowd in the background I had orgotten about this photo. It looks fabulous very movie star styled.

Girls Do IT Too

Sexy calendar deemed out of date

Simon Hayes
Stuart Kennedy

A KEY sponsor for a raunchy calendar promoting women in the IT industry has dropped the product after discovering the front page featured a partially nude woman covered in rose petals.

The Australian Computer Society said the calendar — aimed at raising money to encourage girls to study technology — exploited women.

The calendar includes shots of 20 women IT workers in spoof poses from movies including Dr No, Basic Instinct and Return of the Jedi.

In an email to branch executives, ACS president Philip Argy said he feared the image of a Brisbane web designer in the rose petal scene from American Beauty was inappropriate.

The calendar's creator, Sonja Bernhardt, said she kept sponsors informed on the progress of the calendar.

IT – Page 29

2006- The Australian report on the ACS pulling their calendar sponsorship.

EDITOR'S DESK

The cult of Computerworld (and calendars)

2006 July- ComputerWorld did a follow up story due to the furore created by reactions to the Screen Goddess Calendar.

The picture that appeared in the Cairns Post with the story of the conference sponsor threatening to pull sponsorship if I was a speaker.

Doing IT Around the World Antarctica inside.

Doing IT Around the World Hawaii inside.

Doing IT Around the World Africa cover.

Doing IT Around the World UK Ireland cover.

Girls Do IT Too

Doing IT mention in an influential blog.

Doing IT mentioned in ComputerWorld.

Girls Do IT Too

Doing IT in ARN.

Doing IT in InfoWorld.

Acumen Feb 2008 Million Babes.

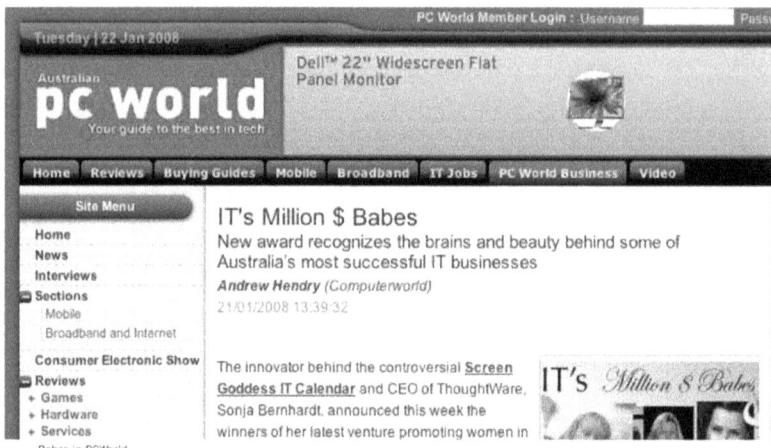

Babes in PCWorld.

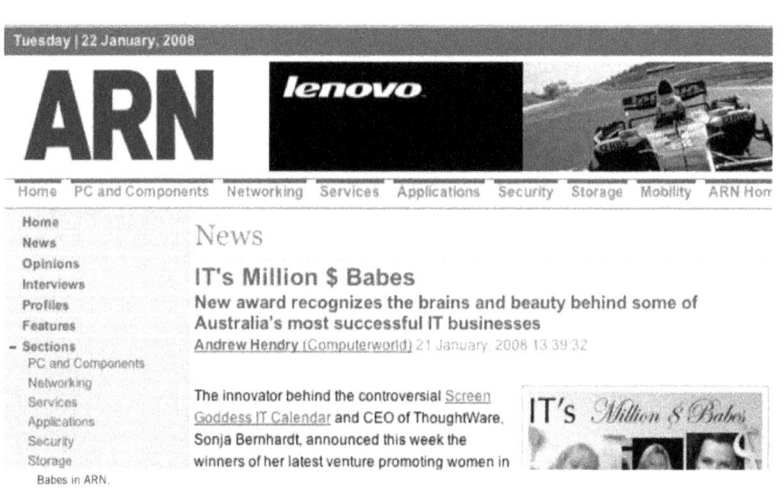

Babes in ARN.

The Butterflies - from the customs incident.

Post the APEC LAC conference at Machu Picchu.

Blockchain book cover.

Gender Inequity Book.

SocialEraCover.

IT Workers. I have a chapter in this book.

I have a chapter in this book.

The Business Build and Growth

Girls Do IT Too

8 The Business Birth and Pivots
Managing Change

> *And the trouble is, if you don't risk anything, you risk even more – Erica Jong*

"Fail Fast and Fail Often."

That's the common wisdom of today. Personally, I hate that saying. I find the terminology and implications are not at all encouraging. Culturally, I believe it sends the wrong message, encouraging people to deliberately act carelessly without accountability, with poorly thought out decisions and errors that lead to failure. I think it is better to focus on what can be done to continue and grow, not to take failure as the "new normal".

I recall an industry event where Liz Manning, then CEO of Software Engineering Australia (SEA), was speaking, and after covering the many unexpected innovations and changes that followed wars, she went on to jokingly say that maybe Australia should start a war with our close neighbours to transform our innovation culture. Well, if declaring war is a bit extreme, the sentiment about dramatic events rings true. Often, whether it is in the political, social, economic or personal realms, key events trigger change.

Both my personal and business lives have seen a few of those triggers that resulted in transformation. Although none were as dramatic as my dad's transformational pivot.

The Dad Pivot

My father grew up as a German living in Germany. In 1944, at the age of 15, he was forced into the Hitler Youth. As so many others, it was a required stage of life, imposed against anyone's personal will. He was thrown into the German war effort on the Russian front – where after a time he was captured and interred in a work camp that extended years beyond WWII. Not exactly a great life for a teenager.

Dad's life back then was full of bravery and daring, but he did not talk about it. Not until my first-born daughter, Naomi, interviewed him in the 1990s for a school project were we to learn of his daring escape from his work camp at a uranium mine. A mine shaft collapsed, and he took advantage of the chaotic situation and, as he expressed it, "shot through to the border". He just ran and ran. The price of freedom when he crossed the border was a further two years' work in a coal mine followed by a release fee. He took that price.

When he returned to his "home life" in Germany he took up house painting and applied to migrate. He applied to both Canada and Australia – and in a stroke of luck for myself and my future existence, Australia's "yes" arrived a day or so before Canada's. Being of strong integrity Dad accepted the first positive offer. So in 1951 he set off as a contract worker to help build the township of George Town in Tasmania.

My father had his share of life pivots, and what transformational moments they were.

I cannot compete with Nazis, war, escape and moving half way round the world to a country with a different language, different customs and former enemies. But my life has had its own key events and transformational pivots. A divorce resulted in me pursuing a career in technology, nearly dying resulted in me finding love and importantly another of life's triggers resulted in me creating my own company.

Each has its own tale to tell.

The Work Pivots

My youthful experiences, along with my wild time at University, early jobs, failed marriage and the creation of WIT helped build me into the person I am. But what was the trigger for me to start my own company? To build my own technology baby from scratch and watch it crawl, then grow?

When it comes to triggers, one with a very loud message is hearing the words "Your position has been made redundant." The careful use of the word "position", not you the person, continues to amuse me. Especially, when it is "you" who is the actual living breathing person departing along with that redundant if abstract position.

In early 1999, I heard those words. I was made redundant from a large technology company, Mincom, an iconic Queensland software firm. Made redundant from Lattice, the role that introduced me to the love of technology and where I had grown my own IT legs.

I had said those exact same words to a number of people in the company in the days leading up to hearing them myself. People I'd worked closely with, and some I'd become friends with. I had spent the previous day with corporate HR watching a number of my close colleagues' concerned and worried faces, as they walked through the door and were asked by HR to sit down. Some were already in tears as by that stage everyone knew what was happening.

As a senior manager of the Lattice business unit, I was sent in as the "bearer of bad news", or perhaps more accurately, the "fall guy". It was my job to tell each person, "Thanks for your work, but as the company needs to rightsize (rightsize not downsize!), your position is no longer available." At which time I always paused, probably more for myself to get a hold on my own emotions and to take a deep breath, then I had been instructed to follow that up by saying, "You are to pack up your personal belongings immediately and a security member will escort you from the premises." My voice broke into tears as I delivered those words. My heart certainly felt the pain.

Then, once that awful job was done, to my surprise I was called into the HR office and made redundant myself. The one concession they gave was that I did not have to leave immediately nor be escorted by security. However, I had to be out within a few hours. Having observed a number of people's reactions to their redundancies, I was aware of the widespread shock and pain that came from such an announcement.

So I rapidly decided that I never wanted that to happen to me again.

At the time I was a 40-year-old single parent of two children, great at my job but hopeless at managing my personal finances. I carried a large debt, and losing my job was a major blow. When I got home the day of the sacking, I let the hot tears fall freely, burning my face as I threw myself on the bed sobbing.

I was upset, desperately upset …

For a day and a half, then I bounced back. Just like my dad.

I knew I was good at what I did and realized that I had no control over the situation. But how could I prevent a repeat sacking experience?

I decided to take it as an opportunity for change, so instead of going back on the job application merry-go-round, I chose to strike out on my own. Within a short time I had set up my own company, ThoughtWare. That way I would be across any company decisions and changes; I would know if a blow was coming and would have control over minimizing or preventing the blow.

Birthing the Company

So Sonja: exit left from corporate life and enter, eyes wide open (or were they shut?), into the world of entrepreneurship.

Originally a consulting and project management firm, the chief asset of ThoughtWare was myself: my consulting skills, project management background and connections. That's how it started, and it quickly brought in income.

At an industry event, I merrily, some might say shamelessly, let people know of my sacking and new company, and let them know my new company was now open for business. I was snapped up for contracting work and the funds started flowing. It really was that easy: I just told the truth and asked for work.

Perhaps the fear of the Y2K "bug" had a part to play in it, but then the IT contracting sector was highly active and attractive. I undertook a number of projects for CITEC, then the Queensland Government technology arm, working there from 1999 to 2001. It was work at CITEC that introduced me to two young men whom I fondly remember and still actively chat with on social media, Malcolm O'Leary and Damian Sheather. I even assisted Mal gather the courage to date the woman who became his first wife. Damian I later hired on and off for contract work. Damian became famous during the 2020 Coronavirus lockdown period, as the chief systems administrator of the internationally renowned Facebook "Bin Isolation Group", where people would dress up for one of the few social outings still possible during isolation time: putting out the rubbish bins.

Damian was and still is a card, technically brilliant but a hard nut who speaks his mind bluntly and openly. Naturally that means many people put him in the too hard category. My main projects at CITEC were with Malcolm, but at one stage I was asked to, "have a look at this very important election system project, because the lead programmer is a problem." That "problem programmer" was Damian, or Damo as I came to know him. After introducing me to Damian, the CITEC representative left, as fast as he could escape, I suspect. I chatted very briefly with Damian, asking him what he thought needed to be done. His ideas were brilliant, but no one else listened to him, some even putting barriers in his way. I could see that with a fixed election deadline looming what needed to be done was not to tie Damian down but to do what he said.

I agreed to take on the project, removed all of Damian's barriers and simply said "Go for it." He did and he achieved the new system on time, with his usual brilliance.

CITEC management were amazed that I had managed to conquer the "difficult person" and manage the project to success. But really all I had done was to let Damian do what Damian knew needed to be done and was immensely qualified to do. That was the start of a style for me that I continued in my own company: respecting and listening to the data analysts and coders and seeking advice from those experts, instead of me assuming I knew what was required.

Sometimes good management just means getting out of the way.

I acquired the nickname of "Cyclone Sonja" at CITEC. It was given to me in an upfront and affectionate way, meaning I worked at incredible speed and rapidly cleaned up whatever the issues were, then swept on to the next. It was a nickname I fully supported and used myself.

From 2001–2004, I was contracted to the Brisbane City Council on a major payroll project. Again, I met some fascinating and lovely people that I remain in contact with today[x]. As the project spread over a number of years and involved quite a few women, many babies were born across that time – nine, I think I counted. We had a baby wall as to us it was almost as if they were part of the entire team, and certainly counted as "deliverables".

In a stroke of luck, or perhaps not for the winning supplier, the negotiating team for the final software selection consisted of three women (myself, a financial representative and a legal representative): all of us pregnant. It was one negotiating team people did not want to mess around with. The winning supplier actually jokingly asked if we deliberately selected three pregnant women as the team. That joke was returned with fierce hormonal frowns.

I tried to hide my pregnancy for the first five or so months, not wanting to go public, given my age, until the amniocentesis results were in. I almost managed it. However, two things were a giveaway to some people who knew me well, and it made them wonder. At that time the project was located in "The Valley" in Brisbane, and on my walk to work I passed pungent food stores and butcher shops. My stomach almost always churned and my eyes watered. Additionally, I was still attending industry events, yet not drinking alcohol. Apparently my *not* drinking champagne at those events was so unusual that some people noticed and wondered why. When I finally announced I was pregnant, those people came forward and laughed, telling me they had guessed.

Being pregnant made me realise how dependent the company was on my physical self, and indeed any person whose individual skills are needed for consulting and project management. I knew that I never wanted to grow the company into a giant monolith. I wanted to keep it small enough to retain warmth with a culture that valued people. But I did need to grow a bit. Having a few consultants under my wing to subcontract out helped a little. It spread the talent and risk. But company stability was still reliant on individual people, and each of these sub-contractor's life circumstances and physical and mental wellbeing. I didn't want to become a "body shop" just farming out work to others. However, it was a start toward diversifying beyond what I could do alone, but more was needed.

I was doing OK taking on consulting work, working on some interesting projects and managing to get up to a six-figure annual income. But it got to a point when I knew I had to transform the company from being dependent on individual people to having a product to sell: so no single failure points that could endanger the whole company if someone was unable to work.

It was time to pivot again. This time to find a product to sell.

Let's Partner

When I had "spare time" from consulting I started looking for products we could sell, as a way to extend my earning capacity beyond direct payment for time worked. Through my voluntary community awards activities, I often came across interesting companies and wondered about becoming involved.

I explored this with a few firms I encountered, but regrettably I spent a lot of time and money chasing down rabbit holes. I always started the process feeling excited and full of hope, but unfortunately it always ended up wasting my time. At one stage we invested a fair bit of time with a promising childcare centre solution, another with a knowledge management system, and another with qualitative data research software. Sometimes with more than one of these at the same time, while I was still contracting out as a consultant. We even dabbled in creating websites, not only for specific clients, but including going down the entire path of building a "babyhub" for parents of newborns where people could, through an individualised but secure web site, share their baby's birth and story with nominated family and friends. This project failed with the same old story, "a lot of interest except when it required spending money".

It was an interesting and very busy time, but it lacked focus and direction. In hindsight it feels like a crazy search for a purpose, throwing darts at every interesting target in sight in the hope something would stick. And in that search, I went down a few rabbit holes. Rabbit holes can be long and winding exploratory paths with many connections and offshoots.

The problem with rabbit holes is they all look so promising when you first dive into them, but as you go deeper the search becomes more and more consuming, while that elusive reward remains just around the next turn. It may take a while to realise you are buried in a hole going nowhere, instead of focusing on areas of greater priority.

Ultimately, rabbit holes are distractions. Maybe it would have been wiser if we had had a rabbit hole time waster litmus test that was applied every few weeks or months. We certainly could have done with testing criteria such as whether the prospect aligned with where we planned to go, and an analysis of whether it was consuming too much time or resources. But perhaps the only proof of what is a rabbit hole and what is the Next Big Thing is only… whether it becomes the Next Big Thing!

Two incidents occurred during that time that still make me giggle.

I always hired people based on the whole person, knowing that roles would evolve to suit that person and their skills. During mid-stage partnering discussions with a Knowledge Management firm, their lead executive "complained" to me that one of my contractors did not look professional enough. When I asked who, he said "Jenine."

I replied, "Umm, really? She always looks and behaves professionally to me."

"She has a nose ring, it *has* to go."

"Jenine has a nose ring?" I was a little shocked. I'd never noticed, or if I had, I'd never registered it as anything significant. It certainly wasn't how I saw or thought of her.

As it turned out she did wear a nose ring daily. Both Jenine and I had a great laugh over how it was so important to him but invisible to me. Postscript to the story: Jenine didn't remove the nose ring, and I didn't proceed with the partnership. There had been other issues that had niggled at me, but the forceful comment that the nose ring had to go, with the implication of "or else", over something so inconsequential to ability, was the last straw for that deal.

The second incident occurred on a day when I had a series of meetings at different buildings in different locations, so had a tightly scheduled day – one of those days where the only way to get through it is to rush, rush, rush. I knew it was going to be an extremely busy day, and I was stressed from the start, knowing I had to dash around from place to place. As I was preparing to leave at the start of the day, my husband, Robin, called out, "Leave your phone on today!"

I didn't understand why. I always turned my phone off when in meetings to avoid distractions and for courtesy reasons. Being asked to leave it on caused me additional stress. What a frustrating day it turned out to be. It was 14th February (a small hint there), and my husband, in an unusually romantic gesture, had arranged for a well-spoken actor to call and recite poetry to me, Shakespeare's sonnet "Shall I compare thee to a summer's day…".

The actor only called me whenever my phone was off. By late afternoon, we'd both had enough of the phone ping pong, and I called my husband expressing my frustration, as the caller had finally just asked me to call him back: which I wasn't going to do. Poor, poor Robin, my ever-patient husband. He tried to mediate, and I finally allowed the actor to call, but by that stage it was no surprise or delight to receive it. It was more, "Shall I compare thee to a raging storm?" than the grand romantic gesture he had planned.

I guess that may explain why overt romantic gestures were not repeated, though there was the time when I tossed aside the crumpled piece of paper in a teddy bear my husband gave me… and the sapphire ring wrapped in it. To this day we still have the poem in our bedroom. We refer to the incident on occasion, laughing at my over-busyness and inability to stop and focus on that special moment, rather than the frustration, then guilt, that I felt at the time.

After a number of genuine but failed attempts to grow my business through aligning with existing products, it became clear that partnering wasn't an easy thing. There were a lot of complications involving personalities and business cultures, including, in my opinion, the need to be philosophically aligned. Therefore, the next step was to make a change: instead of only doing consulting or trying to add someone else's product to what we did it was time to create our own product to sell. To transform what we did.

ThoughtWare evolved into a multiple award-winning software development house. It created Governance, Risk Management, Compliance solutions for the aged care, community care, disability care and Indigenous care space. It was no longer just me and the work I could do personally. It became my saleable asset. I never knew I wanted to be, or even could be, an entrepreneur; it was the redundancy that opened that pathway. If it hadn't happened, I most likely would have continued on in the usual corporate career path. After all, I was good at it, and well paid.

Who would have thought that getting sacked was the best career move ever?

In 2007, a Federal Government publication titled *Women Entrepreneurs: 18 Inspiring Tales of Small Business Success*, wrote a profile on me which begins: "If she ever ran into the man who made her redundant, tech whiz, Sonja Bernhardt would shake his hand and offer him a big thank you."

Are you there, John Hickey? Thank you.

***

Sonja's Tip: Pivoting puts a new turn on life. It doesn't mean it will be easier, just different. But it also doesn't mean it is the end.

9 The Size is Right

From Corporate to Micro to SME

> *When you get into a tight place and everything goes against you till it seems you could not hold on a minute longer, never give up, for that is just the place and time that the tide will turn – Harriet Beecher Stowe*

Evolving into that multi award winning software development house took a number of micro steps, jumping into numerous rabbit holes and some giant leaps of faith. It was fortuitous that I'd done so well consulting, because those funds were necessary later to help seed the company.

The Start

I was in luck, because in early 2005 a mentoring and information program to assist firms to think about what they wanted to do and to prepare a business plan had just been launched, an ideal opportunity to focus our ideas. I applied and was accepted. It was all about business planning. I took three of us out of work, myself, my lead consultant Simone Files, and my son Tom, who had joined the firm, formed the team over those three months. Tom was working with us because earlier he told me that he was at a work crossroads and needed to think about what he did, as he wasn't enjoying the real estate work he was doing and the hours were tough on him. I was delighted to be in a position to leap to his temporary rescue by offering him highly flexible well-paid work so that he could work out his future but still earn while doing so.

With the three of us on the business case, we identified a need for convenient, easy to use software to help businesses in the related strategic areas of governance, risk management, compliance and human resources. The end result was our plan for what would become the ionMy software platform, plus our first two award wins (for Financial Plan and Presentation of Plan). I still remember the bags of money (stuffed laundry bags) we used in the presentation to light-heartedly demonstrate a desired outcome for the business. I still have one of those bags today, with the giant $ sign on the outside. Well that $ goal certainly looked like another rabbit hole many a time, but it did come true in the end. I'm glad that it turned out to be money, not actually bags of laundry.

Maybe there is something in making those wishes concrete. Actor Jim Carrey wrote himself a cheque for ten million dollars, dated for ten years' time when he hoped that he would actually be paid that much. I guess that came true and then some for him too.

Creating a Saleable Asset

Well there we were, with an award-winning plan and a well thought out idea to build some software for an identified market. But how to actually start?

We'd had the company name ThoughtWare since 1999, however right from the start of creating the "product", the "software", the "saleable asset", I wanted to set it up so it could be sold in its own right and separate from the ThoughtWare company itself. That meant giving the software its own identity. Deciding and locking in the name for that hadn't been easy. Having a good name is important. It assists with overall identity and focus and forms part of the overall reputation and history. Plus, we had been advised that to be formal and "real", the name needed to be registered and trademarked. At the time, using the letter "i" at the start of names was popular. So we jumped onto that, as it also had the relevant double meaning of "I" as in "me" and "eye" as in "see and look after", and during the business planning activity we used the working title iHR.

It turned out we couldn't use that name, as when I went to register it, it was too similar to a company in the same category, so our application was denied. We put our heads together and thought of a few others that included ionHR. Where "ion" both sounds like "eye on" and represents the building blocks of life, and HR represented our first ideas for its functionality. At the last minute I decided to drop the HR as that could have potentially limited the functionality. Instead I added the broader "my", so that other functionalities could follow the "my": whether the client wanted to keep their "eye on my people", "eye on my processes", or whatever else of value the core software could support.

Thus I registered "i.on my" (later rebranded to ionMy). Dropping the HR turned out fortuitous, as the software did indeed soon grow far beyond the initial HR focus.

The cost of hiring programmers and technical staff in Australia proved prohibitive, so I explored other options, finally selecting an offshore firm in Sri Lanka for starting the product. That made it far more affordable, frankly, affordable at all. At the time the Sri Lankan price seemed ridiculously low. Simone and I sketched out the idea of the product and it began to be built. That core initial product we sketched out was nothing compared to what the product eventually became. Its initial focus was on HR and for general small business. But as the saying goes, you have to start somewhere.

Simone and I first met when I was working at CITEC in my first contract job after being made redundant from Mincom. We got on well right from the start, and when her work at CITEC finished she joined my company. She was my first valuable representative and remained with us for six years. Around that time, I also applied for a state government grant, and we were awarded $10,000 to help kickstart the software.

In the early stages of creating a product, even small grants like that are highly valuable and make an operating difference. I wasn't taking any salary or payment for my involvement. This is often a necessity in start-ups that are not investor funded.

Simone was a critical part of our early years. As a mother with young children, she reached out to childcare centres and secured us some who signed up as foundation clients. Based on her connections and what she learned from them, I even agreed to having a detailed marketing plan developed and on spending a decent amount of money on early stage marketing. That included a paid spot on *Your Business Success*, a Channel 9 morning television show.

On reflection, while we were very excited by the experience of filming and then viewing our new baby on television, it was far, far too early in our business and product's life to gain real value from that expense. And later, when there may have been value from saying "as seen on TV", the clip was so dated it was no longer suitable.

If I did it again, I probably wouldn't spend so much money up front on mega splash marketing. My experience now tells me that in the world of software you are better off getting a product out there in stealth mode, getting real live user feedback to make it better and more practical, before you do any splash marketing. Maybe that's just me though? Perhaps today's prolific social media already solves this problem and you can maximise marketing without the huge upfront costs? On the other hand, perhaps it is a bit like writing a novel: sure, you can easily, quickly and cheaply get it "out there", but will anyone notice your book among the rest of the throng taking advantage of the same opportunities?

In my opinion, despite how wise or smart the geeks (and I include myself) may feel they are, any valuable software requires user input. And the best input is through use of the product, not just beta testing. Getting something workable into the hands of clients ought to be a top priority, rather than focusing on intensive marketing too early, potentially damaging your future reputation. Or alternatively, waiting to perfect the software before anyone even uses it. Because, let's face it, software can never be perfected. Things change so rapidly that no software can ever be everything or rest on its laurels.

Baby Legs

We began with two ionMy staff, three clients and a five-figure revenue, funded by founder's equity and organic growth. We had zero investors, but we also didn't have any debt. In a classic situation for technology startups, while we didn't work out of a garage, we did work out of my home and certainly did have our first computer server sitting under my desk. Before Coronavirus and a wider realisation that working from home could be both an acceptable practice and of value, we were already setting a benchmark for home and remote working. There was no corporate office, no city address; if required I hired meeting room facilities, otherwise everyone either worked from home or on a client site.

As early as 2001 prior to commencing the ionMy software the company, ThoughtWare, had been recognised as a finalist in the National Work and Family Awards for our flexible work practices. I continued that style of engaging people for all staff who worked on the ionMy software. That style was part of who I had grown to be and was built from my many experiences leading up to this stage.

We spent years without profit, funding the business by injecting founders' own money into it, including income and dividends from my husband's biotechnology business, and selling stock market shares we had invested in previously to top up funds as required. These days running a start up without investor funds is called bootstrapping. It sure takes a lot of faith to keep going and not give up, but luckily for me my middle name is "optimism". I have earned a few other middle names too, like "resilient" and "flexible".

At first the software was for general small business, childcare and schools. Our initial pricing model was far too low, though when weighing the product then versus later, perhaps it was suitable for what we had at the time. That initial price and low client numbers weren't enough to sustain the business without continuing to borrow personal funds. On top of that, after the initial product was developed and delivered from the contracted team in Sri Lanka, the on-going work, maintenance and support was offered out of Australia, which meant more funds were required for more people.

One way to get more funds was to get more clients. We took part in the Queensland Government shared trade stand at the famous CeBIT Tradeshow, where we secured a strategic school site in Sydney. The school's lead Work Health and Safety representative, Lydia Plim, approached our stand at CeBIT. We chatted extensively, as she was bright and had a list of detailed questions, having analysed a number of potential products. To our delight she championed the sale to the school. Our relationship with Lydia remained even after she departed the school and took up consulting work, creating her own company in the field of compliance.

The childcare side was also slowly bubbling along, and it started looking like a winner when ABC Childcare became interested. In a series of presentations and detailed chats with Eddy Groves (owner and CEO), his enthusiasm and interest in proceeding was exciting news for us. I recall his warm smile, firm handshake and comment that "we will do business together." I had previously met Sallyanne Atkinson, who was on the ABC Childcare board, when she was an ambassador in Malaysia and I was there as part of the APICTA activities. I felt comfortable that the deal with ABC was going to proceed. My eyes started sparkling with visions of growth for our future. Then ABC Childcare halted all discussions. What we didn't know was that it was the beginning of their collapse, which was complete by November 2008. And my sparkle died.

We had invested a fair bit into readiness for that sale. The money and time were one thing but, in the end, the personal toll from the hope and lost dreams was another. While I had put everything into that hope bucket, it meant that other areas had either slowed down or halted.

It was time to pivot again.

It was difficult to convince schools of the value of this kind of software, and childcare would be in disarray for some time. I needed to find another sector we could focus on quickly.

It was a casual comment from a colleague, Kim Sheree, that she thought aged care needed help, that reminded me. In our original business plan, one of our potential targets was aged care and community care. Like most business plans, we put lots of work into it, but then when we jumped into the work the plan sat on a shelf gathering dust. After Kim's comment I re-found the plan, dusted it off and yes, the research had shown aged care was a potential market for us.

Kim Sheree has popped in and out of my life since the early WIT days. She stands out to me as a unique and brave person. She is still the only person in a business setting who has told me to be quiet and stop talking. She did this on a plane one day, when my loud voice was annoying or disrupting her own activities, so she, quite rightly, publicly told me to quieten down. It came as a shock, but that shock quickly turned to admiration for her. I hired her on numerous occasions across the years and valued her input and advice. She was, and is, a producer. She rapidly creates quality products and knocks off work at a remarkable pace. Her experience means she provides considered input drawn from multiple sectors.

This pivot needed new marketing and PR as well as researching and understanding the sector's needs. It needed funds, and fast. I had other people working in the company and needed money to pay them, as well as the planned expansion into the aged care sector. It was a make it or break it point, one of a few over the company's life.

I did what I could do and what needed to be done. I put myself back on the market. Luckily, I quickly picked up a well-paying contracting role as a strategist at the Queensland Government CIO department. I worked there from 2008-2009, which helped supply the needed funds for the continuation of my business. Additionally, my loving faithful husband sold his Apple shares, and from time to time we borrowed from our personal account, where his salary and bonus payments from his own biotechnology company were paid into.

He grew to regret selling his Apple shares given the incredible share price increase from 2010 onwards. It wasn't until the sale of my company in 2020 that his regret lifted, because it seemed then to have all been worth it. To have sacrificed then for the later big rewards.

But in the world of entrepreneurs and business, that's an old story.

It wasn't easy balancing the strategist role to deliver a quality outcome, while still running the early stages of my company, but hey: multitasking brings out either the best or worst in us. It mostly meant cramming in extra work on weekends and nights. Plus of course, on top of this I was heavily into industry networking, so carried that load as well. It was a busy, satisfying time that had elements of excitement threaded through it.

The pivot into aged care proved to be wise, with interest from early adopters. It meant I had to go back to the drawing board and review the pricing model. Getting the price right in business is possibly one of the hardest things to do. It took a few years and three different pricing models to find the sweet spot, but at last we did.

I needed more hands on deck, but couldn't afford regular Australian rates, so I worked though the options. Two that turned out to be useful were government-based school traineeships and university-based placements. We engaged a high school trainee, which meant the traineeship was partly funded. The students gained knowledge and real-world experience.

Luckily for me, the first trainee I had, Tiffany, was very smart and efficient at what she did. The traineeship was only a day or so a week, but she learnt rapidly and was highly competent. After Tiffany's traineeship ended, I engaged some others who worked out quite well, but none to the level that Tiffany Hollingsworth did. Move forward a few years and I found Tiffany on

Facebook, she had married and had two young children, and I offered her a job with us. Tiffany ended up working in a wide variety of roles before "settling" into a technology data analyst role with us, where her talent was seriously needed.

The University course-based placement was also very productive. The engagement was considered part of the students' courses and the university proudly promoted the placements, which also meant we received broader promotional exposure. Better than that, we got two talented and innovative students (Natasha Hurst and Shayne Kake), who brought with them great ideas that I approved for them to implement. A good win-win situation where they and I learnt from each other.

Another Australian hiring tactic I used, was engaging a brilliant technical architect who I'd worked at Mincom. Chris Curtis was very kind and offered me affordable rates. Plus, he was so smart and efficient that the time he took to do something was always minimal, so even more affordable. Move forward a few years, and the day Chris told me he could no longer find the time to work with us was the only time I actually cried over the loss of a representative. I actually wondered if we would survive without him. Then I was reminded of a comment a previous manager of mine, Peter, had made, "The cemetery is full of irreplaceable people." Perhaps ironically, that pulled me out of sadness and back to focusing on what I then needed to do.

Using the Right Label

With the product in client hands, we started receiving feedback and realised that to be really useful more development was required, especially around providing clients with further compliance capabilities.

Around this time an industry networking contact, Bob Hayward, headed up Gartner for Asia Pacific. I approached Bob in the hope of tapping into all that Gartner knowledge to help position where and what my product was. He kindly agreed to meet, and I sketched all over his whiteboard, threw in what I thought we were doing and asked for his input. He listened and commented knowledgeably, then said he thought what we were creating was "Business in a Box". Fancy name, but I didn't like it and didn't think it really described what we did, so I kept thinking and researching.

Then I discovered the fledging world of Governance, Risk Management and Compliance, and realised that was precisely our sweet spot. So I labelled the product as GRC. This of course meant we had to remarket the change from Compliance and Competency to GRC, but to me it was worth it, and I was happy to have a recognised, if new, "label" and a focus.

That focus then helped drive ongoing product developments, and also assisted with gathering client feedback with that specific focus in mind. Client use gave us great ideas for functions to add in to the product to help address GRC for them. It became our differentiator.

Business started looking up.

The Toddler Years

From the minute we entered the aged care space, versus the childcare and general business spaces, there was a good match. The sector was feeling significant compliance, accreditation and paperwork pain, and while there were numerous software vendors already in the market, their focus was on clinical care. So we made a splash by offering Governance, Risk and Compliance. We stood out and were ahead of the times with that offer, and interest levels in the new player on the block were high.

Despite that, the take up rate was slow. That suited us at the time, as we needed to learn more about the sector and the optimal way to communicate, address their pain points and price the product. We learnt that many thought of their businesses in terms of cost per bed, a convenient measure of people in their care, so we modified the pricing model to be a rate per bed. This semi-worked, until we started looking at the range of facilities from very small, as little as ten Indigenous clients, to larger sized, which could have thousands of beds and the clients to occupy them.

We also started getting interest from community care organisations, where a per bed pricing formula did not make sense, nor were community care costs and staffing levels per client the same as in aged care. We were sent back to the pricing model drawing board. Well, pricing model spreadsheet, anyway.

There was much excitement as we chased leads and thought about our future growth. It is of interest to note that until then we didn't even have a contract that clients signed onto for the software. We just used handshake agreements. Even our first larger sized chain proceeded without a signed contract. In my over-eager excitement of selling to new sites, I stupidly gave away too much, such as never charging for travel to sites for implementation, even though this could entail significant costs for airfares, accommodation and transport. I would even throw in extra software or consulting services at no cost to the client. I don't know why my husband says my enthusiasm and generosity sometimes override my common sense.

If I had this time over again, I would make sure a lawyer was involved from the start to ensure contracts and agreements were drawn up appropriately. In terms of business and contracts I have discovered it is wise to have it nicely spelt out from the early stages. No matter how much you trust or get along with someone, as people shift in and out of roles or even company ownership changes, general handshake agreements may not be understood or honoured when those changes occur. Even without that, respective memories and understanding of past discussions can prove to be quite different!

After learning some of those lessons I opted to engage a female lawyer (Kay Lam-Macleod) whom I had met through my Women in Technology activities. She was very smart, practical and efficient, did not engage in over legalised speaking, had technical knowledge and made sure things were understandable, and better yet to me, she had her own specialist technology law business. Creating contracts for all clients also revealed the unevenness of pricing among them, as I had to track down the details and document them. This let me set targets to bring all clients in line with the current pricing model and each other, as well as improve our own internal systems. When you are busy running a small, growing firm you have your finger on the pulse, know what you are doing and imagine that your internal systems are consistent and operating well. If you take the time to step back and look, you might find otherwise. But our systems did get better.

The importance of having contracts clearly stating the conditions also applies to staffing arrangements. In the early days people asked for a job, I accepted, and they worked and got paid whatever we had decided: no formal agreement was ever signed. In some cases, I simply asked past work colleagues through social media if they were interested in work, and if they were, we simply agreed a rate and they started. That casualness of engaging people without documentation was later adjusted, when I engaged an HR specialist and formal agreements were introduced.

When you are small, you can engage workers and clients informally and it usually works out fine (but beware running into one of the few cases where it blows up in your face!). However, as you get larger, it just becomes impossible to keep everything straight, and those few problem cases will multiply. At some stage you need to invest in putting things on a more formal basis.

The Getting Of Wisdom

Running parallel to the business baby and toddler years, on the home front we had started monthly philosophy salons. This was where those who were not afraid of discussing taboo subjects like politics, religion and world order, all from an ethical and moral viewpoint, came together to freely bandy around our thoughts and reasoning on a broad range of topics.

We originally started with "brainstarter" topics for people to think about, then made it more focused by presenting on specific selected topics such as the philosophy of interesting ancient cultures, or the ethics of emerging technology, that lead to open discussions. After a few years, we opened up to non-structured discussion topics, then later we just sort of blended into general chat. They were all pleasant events fuelled by food and wine and genuine deep discussion beyond the general daily chatter. I found that it was also a useful avenue to toss in business issues and receive trusted feedback on other experiences. It certainly grounded me in the realities of the world, and I took what I learned into the business.

From time to time some people did take offense at varied viewpoints, however in the interests of freedom of speech and open enquiry I feel it is important to freely express and receive comments without taking offense. Instead it was about hearty, open, honest and meaningful debate. In some ways, given the way the world has now shifted into a very high sensitivity of taking offense, we may have been lucky that our time running these events has finished.

Those early days of structured sessions helped provide content for our semi-retirement cruise ships talks. So even though we stopped holding our regular philosophy salons after almost 20 years, we still gained value from the richness of the discussion, the learnings and the content.

Skilling Up

Skilling the Staff

There was always an offer on the table for those at ThoughtWare to identify training they desired and for that to be arranged. As it turned out, the general day to day of business tended to get in the way of any training happening on a regular basis. External formal training courses and conferences were sometimes undertaken, but not frequently. We did undertake other forms of training and upskilling though. I took out a corporate membership to an online training portal where the technicians could select packets of training as desired. At one stage we ran, via Zoom, internal hints and tips sessions where each person alerted the team things to items of potential interest. We also ran various internal workshops, where we meet face to face and spent a few days covering multiple topics and learning from each other. Some grand face to face workshops were held in Bali and Surfers Paradise, where the added value of being together and sharing knowledge shone through.

Skilling the Clients

I always had the desire to hold client conferences and to establish a user group. I learnt that to do so you really do need a critical mass. In the early days my multiple attempts at this did not produce anything viable.

In 2009 we had a small success with running a virtual conference: remember this was years before Coronavirus changed the events sector overnight. A gorgeous web site was created with a "conference hall" and "break out areas", and presenter material including videos was available for easy access. As discovered during Coronavirus, we had attendees who would not have been able to physically attend a conference but were interested and happy to view presentations remotely. In the end our attendance and viewing statistics were quite high.

It wasn't until 2013 that we had enough critical mass of client numbers to enable success in a face to face conference. So we did one. A majestic conference was held at the Q1 tower on the Gold Coast. Significant organising effort ensured it was a huge success for all. The venue and food were outstanding, and the break out activities such as quick hints and tips sessions proved to be a highlight. The glamorous social event included a magician as an entertainer, and everyone was charmed.

I had dreams of holding more client conferences, however we never quite got there. Similarly, my efforts to kick start an active user group never came to fruition. At one stage I even created a groups-specific website and offered money to fund the group, but a champion to take it on did not magically appear and so the idea did not expand further.

Spreading Our Wings

In 2010 the global technology company NEC was calling. They were keen to get into the aged care act and set up a platform for offering multiple vendor services. The concept was that aged care and community care providers would have one solid technical platform where they could access and use all or parts of multiple software offerings as they needed. It was about advancing the use of cloud computing in the aged care sector; making technology more effective and efficient, so that the cost of delivery was reduced, and aged care organisations could focus more on care, not processes.

We were the first product onto that NEC Aged Care Cloud computing platform. It was easy for us, as our product was already cloud based: to the extent that when Apple's iPads came out, our software operated on them without modification. Often being the most recent product is an advantage, as your technology has leapfrogged those invested in older infrastructure.

The expectation levels for everyone involved with the NEC platform were extremely high. At the MOU (Memorandum Of Understanding) signing agreement with the peak aged care bodies[xi], even the NEC global president and the NEC Asia Pacific president flew over from Japan to attend the event. The event culminated in a delicious special dinner held at the Rockpool restaurant in Melbourne with much handshaking and congratulations all around. My husband and I talked for years about the quality of that meal, which was outstanding, as was the freely flowing wine.

Yet despite the weight and power of NEC's marketing, the aged care cloud concept failed to take off; the sector was not yet really ready for such a brave and collaborative concept. When it was officially declared cancelled and David Cooke (Group Manager, NEC Australia) advised me, I shot back, "Oh well, Dave at least we got an amazing meal and evening and some branded coffee cups out of it!"

And that was the end of that. Despite significant planning and resources invested, nothing happened. The only lesson I could take away from that was even all the money in the world, high profile support and a great idea is no guarantee of success if the time isn't right.

Outside of aged care, in 2009 we teamed up with an accounting firm and a legal firm to provide our software for free to 1,000 companies, as part of a small business stimulus package. The accounting firm was B-free (a pre-Xero-type online software) and the legal firm was Legal ToolBox. This initiative generated a lot of initial interest, but it went on to prove the old saying that people only value what they pay for. Being offered for free meant many did not value the solutions, especially when any governance requires added workloads for no direct revenue, so it didn't work well for any of the firms involved. Plus, another downside of giving things away is that paying clients then consider they are paying too much.

At the time we thought it was a great idea, to assist and offer services for free, both as a community support activity and in the hope of a stream of tail revenue in subsequent years, but it didn't work out that way. There may be a reason why some sayings have been around for years. In the excitement and desire to assist I ignored that people only value what they pay for.

My baby had started to grow and learn. It was time to nurture it further.

***

Sonja's Tip: It's much harder to commercialise than you think: it takes more time, money, effort and internal strength than you ever plan. As a guide I suggest double the time and at least triple the cost you estimate. Then do that again!

10 Growing Pains

Developing Resilience

You may have to fight a battle more than once to win it –
Margaret Thatcher

The terrible twos to the troublesome teens can be considered to be the middle years of your business. They may last a shorter or longer time than in a human life, and encompass the period after the excitement and energy of start-up and before sustainable financial and market stability. For us it spread across a number of years and was as much a roller coaster ride as is bringing up a human child. Full of tantrums, growing pains, compromise, and letting go.

Technical Tantrums

"Sonja, you there, I'm sorry to have to tell you but something critical has happened."

That Friday in March in 2010, I was driving back to the home office after dropping my daughter at school when I got *the call* from my chief architect advising that there was no contact with our server. Then we discovered that the relationship between the person we dealt with and the firm he used had fallen down. We had no access and more importantly our clients, some with critical needs, could not access our system.

Our server provider had disappeared overnight.

Disappearing server providers is the stuff of technical nightmares. This was our third provider if you exclude our own in-house hosting under my desk at the very start. Our first "real" provider was a major corporate data centre in Sydney, where we started small then thought we needed to progress to a dedicated server. However, the costs of upgrading to that early in our business were just too much, so we swapped to a local server provider on the Gold Coast, who I now refer to as "the cowboy".

As that nickname might indicate, we quickly moved away from them to what seemed like a good in-between solution, a medium-sized established firm in Brisbane at a recognised data centre... but then they disappeared. Well *they* didn't, and certainly their lead person, who I knew from industry networking and was recognised and respected, didn't disappear but went onwards and upwards.

Unknown to me though, he had outsourced the server to someone else, who then disappeared. A few lessons for all there, such as mates may be mates, but don't assume because you know someone that you can apply less scrutiny to the contracting. Engage lawyers early, and value their review of contracts and learn to ask if the services provided are outsourced or subcontracted.

Now I tend to be a positive, optimistic person but also one who faces reality: hope for the best but be prepared for the worst. So between the strong language I felt like expressing about the disappearing server, and I'm sure I did, and the tantrum I felt like throwing, I also thought hey, what a great opportunity to see if our disaster recovery plan works.

Without covering all the details – it did – *eventually*. Luckily a data backup had been taken at five that morning and stored on our own server, and of course our software was securely stored off site. Thank goodness it was Friday, as not only did I and the chief architect need a drink, but we found we had holes in our recovery plan, and it took myself and two other people (thank you, Chris and Mark) all weekend to finally get it all sorted. But the end result was this: our clients only lost Friday access – and we then had an infallible recovery plan that we knew worked.

Perhaps it's true that whatever doesn't kill you makes you stronger.

Those were the early days for cloud computing, but thanks to some forward thinking and our solution being new, not embedded in older infrastructure, our entire architecture was cloud designed. So being armed with the "spoils of the disappearing server war", such as an improved build-from-scratch plan that we knew worked in the real world, made it easier for us to have confidence that we could expand onto other cloud platforms, such as the emerging Microsoft Azure and Amazon Web Services (AWS) platforms. If we weren't cloud-enabled, we would have been unable to swiftly arrange a new server/host and via remote access get back to business as usual. As for our clients, the real users – well, to them all they noticed was that one day out of service. Whew!

Whew to being ready and having made early-stage wise decisions to build in new but promising technologies. Not that investing in "new" is always the best strategy. Sometimes today's "new" is not tomorrow's "new normal" but its "what?" But in this instance my chief architect had years of knowledge and had deeply analysed the facts, and it was his advice I took for the underlying architecture.

Product functionality? Well that was an entirely differently set of experts.

Growing the Product

In truth when our base product was initially completed by the Sri Lankan contractors it was very, very basic. It operated without obvious bugs but was limited in what it actually did. To use the modern jargon, it was far from "feature complete".

That didn't stop my pride in having my own product designed and developed from scratch. At least there was a product and it was out there being used. But to grow in the marketplace it needed to become more, lots more than how it began. Time to nurture that product, which meant time to put on the thinking caps. Everyone in the company had different and interesting ideas about new functions and features, which areas to prioritise, how to select the right ones, how to know which ones to invest in and focus development efforts on. We could not afford to do all at once, in terms of either available resources or money. Decisions, decisions, decisions.

The pain of making those decisions led me to my brainchild on how to grow the product functionality. I decided to tap into the most knowledgeable experts available: to ask the people using the product. To put aside our own ideas and to seek input from the customer base. It worked brilliantly. I offered clients free development of any great idea that enhanced the overall product, as the value of their idea was recognised.

The norm in the software industry is to charge, often like the proverbial wounded bull, for product enhancements and client suggestions. We went against that norm and were impressed by the superb ideas that came out of our client base. If an idea was specific to only the one client or was required in a set timeframe rather than slotting into our own schedule, then it fell into the usual pay for development mode, but outside of that we developed our product roadmap based on client ideas and inputs. For many years the statistics on our development clearly showed that more than 80% were from client suggestions and on the equally great side less than 10% were bugs (the remainder being our own enhancements). It also meant we began to rapidly learn more about the sector.

As part of this I also decided to not have customised versions, and instead have one product, one solution. We never officially adopted a specified methodology such as Waterfall or Agile but did a combination: feature driven from client requests; semi-agile in that the client gave iterative feedback as it developed. Instead of full-blown multiple specifications, we either worked directly from a development ticket, or attached to that ticket was a mini-specification. In all cases development was rapid. I liked to think of us as a hybrid development house, using our flexibility to develop in a way that suited what was being created. What a way to ensure the product grew by having capability that was practical and needed. On the downside, it meant we rarely made money for developing the product. But in the long run it meant that the product, and in particular the process flows and integration across the multiple areas, was strengthened, and this became one of its strong defining factors.

Once at a client's request, I weakened, and let them not upgrade but remain on an older version of our software. They were a fairly large organisation going through multiple organisational and technical changes, and they didn't want to add any more to the mix. That meant we had two products to support, and as time moved on and more upgrades were released to the main version, their product fell more and more behind; including not upgrading to the new user interface we'd introduced to keep up with the technical times. Supporting the older version also became more difficult, as the call centre was trained in the latest version and not the older one.

Then, surprise, surprise, the client started to complain that their software was outdated. And thus began a spiral of dissatisfaction. We almost begged them to upgrade, but as their original technical lead person had left and new people came in who didn't know why they were still on an older version, their complaints were about the older look and feel and how they now had a large upgrade job ahead of them. All the fault of the vendor, of course. Regrettably, we eventually lost that client, and I believe it could have been avoided if I hadn't weakened and they had stayed onboard with the latest product.

Sometimes you really have to be strict and stick to rules. Bending them, thinking you are being kind and assisting, may have the exact opposite effect. Nobody will thank you for it after the first week, but they will certainly blame you for any problems that result for the rest of time. I also think that if we had been a giant corporate, the client would never have pushed to not upgrade: they would have just known and accepted that they were to keep in line with the software or accept the consequences. So in some ways I fell into a trap of being small and letting others treat us as such.

Never give in! Never surrender!

Over-Flexibility and Compromise

At the core of my approach is the belief in the individual as a thinking adult, and their ability to be smart and provide valuable input. Implicit trust that staff are committed to their work and would deliver desired outcomes was part of my employment philosophy. I hired on the person and their skills, with the strong belief that a role would form around them, which often meant that individuals would decide the title of the role they desired. Through applying this the company gained a reputation for smart operations among both staff and clients, as it translated to innovation in processes. Staff realise that enhancing a process to be more productive, or creating templates for activities, means that their job would be done in a more efficient manner and timeframe. That meant they would still be paid for completion but would "score" time flexibility. In addition, clients got to benefit from repeatable, consistent practices, and streamlined costs.

One area that greatly benefitted from this approach was the implementation process. Due to my project management background we had adopted a methodology that was a mixture of the classic PMBOK™ (Project Management Body of Knowledge) and also the PRINCEII™ (PRojects IN Controlled Environments) Methodology, thus we used a hybrid tailored from my own experiences. Over time the tool set supporting this methodology grew as staff creatively improved or created new tools to support the process, making their lives easier and adding professional polish and efficiency to our implementation process.

We were actively engaging in work from home and flexible arrangements long before Coronavirus lockdowns forced many people to work from home. We set benchmarks for extremely flexible working conditions.

By so doing I also learnt the downside of flexibility, a downside I expect others may discover in the future as work from home increases post Coronavirus experiences. To my utter surprise some people just do not like working from home. They are not comfortable with it, and not necessarily because they lack a home office, but because they like being surrounded by people, or in some instances because they lack self-discipline. One person I hired disliked working from home so much she would go to the local library just to be among people. She would sit there and work. I always saw working from home as a benefit, a bonus, a delight. And from a business point of view, it saved money on office rentals and equipment, which was highly attractive for a small company.

Working from home locations did not mean there was no team environment. We collaborated on projects and activities and met as a team via the web meeting room for regular catch ups and also via our web-based newsletter for shared news. Additionally, we arranged social face to face catch ups and meetings at restaurants and coffee shops, which in many ways felt extra special as you didn't meet face to face on a daily basis.

Part of our flexibility wasn't just where to work from, it was also hours worked. Treating people as adults, I let them decide their work hours. This worked well for most. For example one person loved to play golf, and was looking at becoming a professional golfer, so he arranged his working times to be outside of day golf hours. A bonus from flexible times for the organisation was that as no one was full time, it gave us room to quickly expand overnight within existing resources, by stretching a little further without over stretching and over stressing. This "bought us time" while we sought out other people with suitable skills to help support growth times. Generally, people don't mind a small stretch of extra work occasionally. It's the long term, endless pushing that causes issues and burnout.

Ahead of our time, we even conducted client presentations and support using a secure web-based meeting room. This meant people in roles such as consulting or business analysis did not even need to leave their home to professionally present to a prospect or client. The concept of using an interactive, collaborative web meeting room was not only to create greater flexibility for ThoughtWare and the prospect or client, but it was cost and time efficient, and also environmentally friendly, by reducing road and plane travel. Despite that though, we discovered that in the end prospects and clients both expected and preferred face to face meetings.

Often, we conducted the remote meeting then had to follow it with face to face, so ultimately it didn't result in any savings and consumed more time. Again, maybe post Coronavirus such expectations will have changed, and remote presentations will be considered professional and acceptable, perhaps even preferable.

One coder rapidly grew to appreciate the flexible lifestyle we offered. She was receiving up to three times her country's average salary for that kind of work, and was able to work from wherever she desired, at times that suited her. This translated into some years where she would spend part of the year in Europe, working for us when not exploring, enjoying lengthy family holidays while continuing to work at times that fitted in and around her family activities.

Sounds great doesn't it? And it was… for her. Meanwhile, back at the ranch, coincidentally(?), we all began to notice a decline in her work standard and response times. While she genuinely meant to be as productive as usual, it just didn't really transpire, plus I was starting to become a little concerned about the potential lack of security around her holiday internet connections. Mix that in with her perhaps losing a bit of appreciation for the incredible flexibility that was being provided, and expecting even more, leading to potentially abusing the "system". As a result, I decided that even though working from home was an entrenched work practice within in the firm, it was time to open a formal office and take the coders off working from home and into an office environment.

That took us to another level.

We hired a room at a fully serviced office space in Bali. It was great, as the arrangement also gave us access to hundreds of ad hoc offices around the globe, including at airports and office facilities throughout Australia that we could tap into when required. It also brought the coding team together, which proved to be more productive. Our Fiji team had always worked from rented offices, so in the end only the Australian arm worked from their homes or from Head Home Office…or libraries and the like.

People are individuals. Some thrive with the extra responsibility and flexibility of working remotely. But others are grateful for working from home for a month, then accept it as not only the new normal but the baseline – wanting more for less. Other types of workers seem to thrive more with the synergy of personal contact. No one size fits all.

Alliancing

After the earlier futile attempts at sourcing a partner, I still clung onto some hope of growing through aligning with other firms. As I'd done in the early days we tried a few different prospects without any taking root and growing.

Some were rather exciting and introduced a few in my company to the corporate world. At one stage, a bright, community-minded consultant turned up. I had originally met her when I hired her as a university-based project representative when I was managing a large project for Brisbane City Council (and later re-hired her into that project a few times). She, Abby Kamalakathan, had gone on to have a shining career and was now working for one of the large consulting firms. They were keen to strengthen their aged care representation, and she invited us in for talks to explore the alliance possibilities.

We had a series of exciting meetings, and again my eyes shone with the future possibilities. Alas, it didn't amount to any real sales or market expansion for us. It did help us tune our message and refocus on marketing material, but did not produce any commercial activity – apart from one client that we brought to the alliance prospect and they conducted some consulting for. For a short while some of us enjoyed putting on our corporate clothing and meeting in giant city office towers and having a peek into corporate life.

Abby continues her career rise and in 2019 I was delighted to be invited to her wedding reception.

Using my never-ending optimism and built-in resilience we also formed an alliance with a large international player in the aged care software supplier space. They were well funded and were seeking to expand their operations in Australia after having successfully grown through alliances overseas.

Through my involvement in the Aged Care IT Vendors Association (ACIVA), I had a decent relationship with the potential alliance company's newly appointed General Manager, so I approached her with a view towards adding our product to their marketing base.

We tried to schedule a meeting, but naturally she was mega busy establishing their Australian base. Between her schedule and mine, with her based in Sydney and me on the Gold Coast, and both of us travelling a lot, it was getting rather difficult to find a shared open timeslot when we were in the same city. So back to the meeting drawing board I went and rethought about how I could make this meeting happen, as I wanted to talk in person not just remotely. I decided to make things easier for her, so when she was on a flying visit into Brisbane, I picked her up from the airport and drove her to her VIP meeting, talking the entire way. To her credit she listened, agreed and actioned my ideas by proposing to global headquarters that we become their partner in Australia for Governance, Risk and Compliance. They agreed. This was a promising start and ultimately may have become a good alliance. However, the sale of my company occurred before any substantial commercial activity from the alliance became fruitful.

Well, not quite true. We did receive the go ahead from one company they introduced us to, and we commenced early stage implementation activity, but then without warning the client company pulled the plug leaving us high and dry. Later it was revealed the company had some financial and people issues and had made some serious cutbacks, including our project.

That wasn't the only company which had agreed to go ahead with us then pulled out. Once, after multiple demonstrations, numerous trips to their corporate offices, costing us money for each trip, and responding to a tender, I was informally advised in an email that we had got the deal and the paperwork was on its way. We celebrated within the company. However, the paperwork never arrived. I patiently waited a few weeks, when on reflection I probably should have got onto it rapidly and not allowed delays.

It turned out that the client company had had a change of leadership, and the new CEO had put in place a "freeze" on any in-transit arrangements. He then decided to cancel the agreement with us, and instead installed a product he was familiar with from a prior organisation: a product that had never made the shortlist nor been demonstrated. I spoke to my lawyer about it, but we decided we just had to think of it as bad luck for us, as trying to pursue the deal further could lead to damaged reputations for them and us. So I had to let it go and keep moving forward. Another case where I wondered whether they would have treated a large company in such a fashion.

Delegating – Learning To Let Go

Phone, Wallet, Keys, Phone, Wallet, Keys; the Adam Sandler skit repeats to remind people of what not to forget. In my business that chant translated to Travel, Accounts, HR. I originally undertook those functions, but ultimately all had to go, and be handed over. I needed to end each business day without worrying about them consuming my time.

It was time to let go of my CEO and founder's ego, and the frequent feeling that only I could do it, or more correctly only I could do it the way I wanted it done. It was time to bite the financial bullet and hand over day to day operations.

Looking after travel bookings started to consume far too much of my time. The flights, the car hires, the accommodation and so on; and when there were delays and changes required, it became downright painful and a nuisance for me to manage. There wasn't enough travel-associated work to employ someone, but it was too much for me on top of my other activities. Enter Corporate Traveller, the corporate travel management company. How marvellous that turned out to be. It lifted a huge weight off my shoulders, I wished I'd started with them earlier than we did. It also made accounting for travel easier, as their systems fed into our accounts making reconciliation of expenses so much easier. We all grew to feel that our Corporate Traveller lead representative, Cassie, was part of our team. We certainly shared celebration events with her.

With our bookkeeping and accounts I had tried a few options, hiring consultants, rotating doing the accounts between my husband and myself depending on who was the busiest at that time, my mum even looked after them for a while. Then finally, as business picked up and the volume of transactions increased, I bit the bullet and decided to outsource the entire function. To do so I swapped from MYOB to the funkier, newer Xero. The migration was easy and I engaged a Xero outsourcing firm to manage our books. That worked a charm. Their attention to detail was far greater than mine and they managed to sort out inconsistencies and discrepancies. And my time was freed up.

There is that old saying that it is better to spend time *on* the business rather than *in* the business. I was aware of that, but daily practices, and a lack of profit, meant I spent lots of time in the business. Outsourcing came at an affordable price with the enormous benefit of released time for me.

HR is something I probably should have outsourced from the start, though it never occurred to me as our hiring practices were informal and through people we knew. But in the end, I think that distancing the engagement and induction process from myself may have had advantages. Plus, in my experience, as soon as you get even a handful of people working together, HR issues begin to emerge. Luckily, I located a highly economical local HR consulting firm that then relieved me of needing to look after day to day HR issues.

This was later in the company's life and on reflection was something I could and should have had in place long before hand. My company has hired almost 100 people over the years, some with times as short as a few months and some employed for more than a decade.

I started to learn that delegation was indeed a great skill to acquire.

Chasing Sales

"Build a better mousetrap and the world will beat a path to your door", is a phrase attributed to Ralph Waldo Emerson in the late nineteenth century. Perhaps true back in the 19th century but certainly not true for the 20th and 21st centuries. Getting to, staying in and growing your market is simply hard work.

Sure, there are the occasional incredible ground-breaking products or trends that enjoy whirlwind success, but for the vast majority it's work, work, work.

We tried a whirlwind merry-go-round of all the usual techniques of traditional advertising, trade show attendance, sponsorship of events, conference speakers, tender applications, awards, internet campaigns, publishing case studies, thought leadership articles, the lot, including my own sector volunteer activities. We adopted smart techniques of using unique contact details with each advertisement, campaign and trade show so we could measure the effectiveness of each. We offered clients incentives to introduce others to the company, and we hired sales experts. With great expectations I purchased guides and books from "experts" in these fields and put their tactics in place.

When one failed, we just as enthusiastically and hopefully went on with another. To me it all seemed hit and miss, but on reflection I do admit we were hit and miss ourselves, not applying adequate consistency or sticking to the plans. Maybe if we had stuck with our drawn-up marketing plans for each month we would have grown faster sooner? I don't know. Marketing is still a little mysterious to me. You never really know what will work and what won't. It almost has to be multi-pronged, with perhaps a repeat of earlier approaches just in case anything has changed since that strategy was last attempted.

I was always trying to find that magic marketing bullet that would shoot us to the top. The chase is full of excitement and is certainly a rollercoaster ride with so many ups and downs. Unfortunately, our most consistent experience was that no matter how well a marketing or sales consultant presents themselves, what they are really good at selling is… themselves!

The secret I think is just staying in there, being resilient. More often than not, success appears to be more a matter of luck or being in the right place at the right time. All the smart plans in the world don't change that. So you keep plugging on, trying and re-trying, until you hit that magic combination of formula and moment.

Resilience: Hair Today, Gone Tomorrow

There was a buzz in the air, we were excited. Perhaps we did have a better mousetrap, after all. We had been sent a closed tender, meaning the opportunity to apply had only been extended to a few selected firms. It was for a giant multi-functional chain in the aged and community care space. They had found us by scanning trade shows, and their pre-analysis had put us and only one other company on their list.

We spent hours and hours, in fact over 150 hours, responding to that tender over a two-week time period. I designed a new style of response, various staff members provided their input and I collated the responses, ensuring all questions and parts of questions were responded to, with evidence provided such as screen shots and sample reports. It was reviewed and reviewed and finely tuned. It was gorgeous. Everything was responded to and the level of fit was very high.

Submit!

We were invited to demonstrate to a team of the state and operational managers from the prospective organisation. It was very exciting, as this was our first giant chain and would make a significant difference to us and them. Demonstration preparations were thorough, the software database was even set up to reflect their nomenclature and examples. So much effort and hope went into that. Then two of us trotted off to Melbourne to present.

The demo seemed to go well, with all scenarios working perfectly; we even had alerts set up and working to demonstrate how powerful receiving compliance messages to your phone or computer was. The two of us felt that even though a couple of people did not seem enthusiastic at the demo, the rest did, and we knew the software and the associated real time reporting was impressive.

We lost the deal!

I had been advised that our price was spot on and that the tender response was outstanding, that they had never received any of a similar quality. The prospective company's coordinating person told us the reasons we did not secure the deal were as follows.

Our demonstration style was too folksy and friendly, and should have been more "corporate". There were too many alerts and reminders going off and no one wanted that much happening. The worst reasons were that the demonstration team was only female and there were no males (and this was said in 2014!), and neither of those females had corporate hair. Those last two reasons were outrageous, and luckily, I'm not a litigious person.

In the end all those reasons can be interpreted as saying we lost the contract on a perceived lack of credibility. Despite all the sector work and real credibility we had, we failed to show that at the demonstration.

I heard the winning team was three men in suits that spent a lot of time on establishing the credentials of their firm and a small amount of time on the product. I also bet their team of all one gender was not seen as a weakness. Sigh.

Interestingly, nothing much has changed in the corporate world since the old catch-phrase "nobody lost their job by buying IBM", meaning a conservative purchase from a known corporate is a safe move. Those who rise through the ranks of traditional corporates, often can't think outside that box.

Even today I am still sad about that lost opportunity, but what do you do… Pick yourself up and get back on with it. Learn and later laugh (maybe) at the experience.

All was not lost though, as that tender response later morphed into our standard tender response. We added company credential slides to the PowerPoint presentation, or "slide deck" as they're now called. We limited future demo alerts down to no more than three so as not to frighten the natives, and in significant future demos we invited in a *token* male, usually my husband. Folksy and friendly… well that was difficult as it's my personality and the way I engage an audience. And hair, well… far too subjective to deal with.

Hello, How Are You?

As we grew and had representatives in other continents, it became harder to know what was going on in the multiple areas and with each representative. I tried many different ways to communicate within the company. We had internal electronic newsletters, which came and went, as the effort to do them was significant and by the time they were compiled the news was old news. We used Skype for quick messaging and highlights.

However, I felt that more formal communications were required. We started what were termed DIO's. Day In Office – where individuals spent one day a month or so in at Head Home Office with me. The day always commenced with a chat based on a pre-delivered status report. Then the staff member did their usual work and addressed anything that cropped up as we spoke. For staff overseas we did similar days remotely and over a shorter time period.

These meetings were reasonably successful. There was still a problem though, in that we didn't have any formal group communication. We tried to do that remotely and set a regular monthly meeting chat with everyone but it didn't really work. The chats dragged on, and I know some people just wanted to get back to work and not listen in to an area they were not really involved. Besides, a month comes around really quickly.

Many years before, when I was managing a project with dozens of people on the project team across multiple functional groups, I started early morning stand up meetings where very quick updates were given by each team on what they were working on that day and week. We called them Stuppies – stand up meetings. They had a set timeframe that we stuck with and everyone had no more than 2 minutes to summarise. These were brilliantly successful. Agile development processes weren't really in at that stage, however it was sort of an early agile process. Maybe I should have done the same within my own company.

***

Sonja's Tip: In business and life, you can get knocked sideways. All you have to do to get up one more time than you are knocked down.

Girls Do IT Too

11 Follow the Money

Where Did the Money Go?

Money is only a tool. It will take you wherever you wish, but it will not replace you as the driver – Ayn Rand

Money, Money, Money

Oh, the money I wasted! The pain of hindsight, knowing that some funds could have been saved and not spent or wasted. Alas hindsight is exactly that… hindsight, and not available to you at the time. The things you would do differently with knowledge you gain later. Unfortunately, the time machine isn't invented yet.

In many ways I was hopeless at two things. One was closely monitoring the money, the other was, despite my earlier sales experiences, that I sucked at being able to close a deal.

I have a generous, open nature and tend to be impulsively over-generous with time and money. This manifested itself in the business with deal closing, where it meant I stupidly jumped in and gave too much away too soon, which both undervalued the product and services and resulted in less revenue and more costs. I tried and tried and tried to engage deal closers over time, but the only deal they seemed able to close was for me to hire them.

The company's history has a string of failed attempts at engaging "hotshot" salespeople. It is true that marketing, presales and sales closers are all very different skills, and you do need all three and not one person who is good in one of those areas and weaker in the others. Two out of three may not be bad, but it is probably best to seek at least three people for the specific skills. In an attempt to mitigate the gap between the cost of hiring those people and the sales success I introduced a commission-based approach, where part of the payment was a reasonable base and the rest a high percentage commission. However no one I approached was willing to bet on themselves enough to agree to that type of renumeration package.

Internally my generosity meant I rewarded staff with extras. Of course, usual business expenses, meals out and celebration events were funded, but I always included extras. For one young starter I paid for her first business outfit, for a few others I funded holidays and mini breaks away. Once, when attending a business workshop/conference in the USA, I funded a holiday for a technical staff member, who loved theme park rides, to stay at Disneyworld for a few days plus a trip to New York. That same person scored a holiday or two to the Gold Coast to have fun in those theme parks as well. I paid for another staff member and her partner to have a holiday in Fiji, and previously a holiday in the USA.

Finding what an individual values as a reward is a lesson in itself. It is not always money, often it is as simple as recognition and praise for work done, or time off.

Not that I followed this advice myself. I paid people that I hired directly, instead of from an agency or outsourcing firm, above the average rates for their country. Often, their rates when they commenced were a little above the average, then I increased the rate. Being paid above average sounds good, though on refection I think having a frequent review process with incremental payment increases may have been wiser. I was surprised once when a staff member said, "Yes, I know I receive at least twice what others do for this type of role, but I haven't had an increase for two years!"

They'd also enjoyed gifts and bonus payments, but it was true that their base rate had not changed in that time. That comment threw me, because to me being paid more means you already have more. So much for my system of paying an above average baseline with ad hoc increases being valued. Stability and a visible incremental pathway seemed to be more what people were after.

How quickly yesterday's generosity becomes today's new, expected normal and tomorrow's "what's next?".

From a client's point of view, my generosity meant I would provide added extras. One year I engaged a local artist to do some stunning art works as gifts for clients. For a few years I had flowers, gourmet baskets and chocolate packages delivered, and another year I gave away iPads to key clients. The gift giving was inconsistent and uncoordinated, and I'm not sure it made any real difference in the clients' perception of us. If I was to do this again, I would make it a structured plan where the gift giving was based on achieving specific business outcomes, instead of impulsively as the idea arose.

I learnt some other lessons around this too. One was to spread this gift giving, or at least knowledge of it, beyond any single contact at a client firm, because people can be career mobile and move on, and the history of the relationship goes with them, making the gift giving even more irrelevant. Plus one lesson I consistently failed to learn was that the more you tend to give away the more people expect it as "normal" and the less they seem to appreciate it.

Outside direct benefits to staff and clients, it is so easy to get carried away by a wave of other "things" that end up consuming time and money. Another extra money spend the company undertook was sponsorship of a variety of events and activities, such as GovHack (GovHack is a hackathon styled event where technical teams work with Government data sets to create a new service), and also supporting people who I knew were great speakers with valuable information to pass on. I would sponsor them to be speakers at aged care conferences, funding their travel and paying their speaker fees so they were encouraged to be there and were able to spread their great knowledge.

Again, I'm not sure of the measurable benefit of some of these activities. Certainly, there was a "feel-good" benefit for us at the time, but perhaps these types of extras need to be more carefully considered before over-enthusiastically diving into them. Mostly they can be fun and have a community-minded feel, which are important. Ultimately it ought to be about working out a balance, or at least a set of performance and benefits indicators before just diving in and doing them. What is petty cash and time for a multinational company can really eat into the cash flow and time of a small, growing business.

From 2013, at the start of each year I produced an annual report of the previous calendar year. Even though we were not publicly listed I felt it was a good exercise and was useful for reflection purposes. Besides, January and February were traditionally quieter months so I had the time to look inwards. The reports were confidentially shared throughout the company and covered statistics such as trade shows, leads, demos, sales, clients, product development and support, as well as expected financial indicators. This information was always interesting and led to shock at the results or wow moments where we were doing better than we had thought.

If I was to run another small business, I'd probably have a money person on board, either on an advisory board or as a CFO, and maintain stricter governance regarding spending authorisation. It is too easy to get lost in the day to day running of a business and be blissfully unaware of a looming crunch… perhaps especially when the CEO is overly endowed with optimistic enthusiasm.

On at least two occasions I openly advised staff of an upcoming dire financial situation and that we needed to tighten our belts, as the cash flow did not support the monthly mandatory payments, including their own. Everyone's work and time was needed so we couldn't look at reduced hours. Instead the chief tactic that we agreed on adopting was delayed payment to staff, with full repayments when funds became available, as it was *just* a cash flow issue, where time was needed for the cash to flow again. We worked well together, each person worked out their mandatory minimum financial need, and payments were reduced to that with the difference "banked" for later repayment.

It worked.

In some ways, maybe the higher payments people received and the flexibility we provided, helped build the loyalty that came into play when this type of tactic was needed. Working together on the issue, instead of against each other or at odds, it certainly created a feeling of a cohesive company. We were working together, and all of us believed that things would improve. And they did.

Learning to Economise

I really need to learn to control my generosity. All that crazy impulsive over-generosity to people meant that I needed to economise elsewhere when it was possible.

Activities I undertook to try to economise included using web-based graphics firms for marketing materials. This certainly saved money, however looking back I believe it meant we had disparate, disconnected material. It wasn't until much later, when we engaged a professional marketing firm, that everything came together. Sometimes it's not until you look across everything that you see that while individual parts may look good in isolation, as a whole they just don't come together. Which in turn means your marketing message and images are not consistent.

Perhaps for marketing I should have paid more attention to my MBA training about the Gestalt Theory that states that the whole is greater than the sum of the parts.

Another traditional marketing activity we undertook was giving out promotional items at demonstrations and for trade show goodies. There is such a wide variety of items to purchase, and many only come in lots of 1,000 or more. Additionally, we, our prospects, and clients tended to get tired of the same trinkets year after year, so we kept adding more to the mix by introducing a new item every year or so. Our changing logo and colour scheme also meant that we had old stock that had to be used up. In my experience the best items we purchased over time were the smaller practical ones, such as screen wipes and magnifiers. Though in the end I question the real benefit of such giveaways. People tend to flock to stands to grab the goodies, but does that result in richness of contact?

Then again, it is marketing. One of those things you have to have, but how do you ever know what parts did any good? You keep trying until you hit something that works, and the last thing you did gets all the credit.

I also elected to outsource other capabilities such as phone answering. The phone had been bothering me for a while, as it meant I was on tenterhooks in case it rang, since the 1300 number was directed to my home phone. So I never knew if it was a personal or business call, and also I could not eliminate the background noises of regular household activity. The day I was waiting anxiously for a reasonably sized organisation to call me back at home, I decided to seek a better yet affordable option.

Solving the problem was easy. I located an Australian firm, Greymouse, who provided remote services out of Fiji. They offered reception answering services using perfectly English-speaking staff for extremely affordable rates. They quickly discovered what type of calls we had and crafted words to use in response. Within a day or two we were all set up and I was able to be less stressed and distracted over the phone. The arrangement worked brilliantly. Part of Greymouse's process included regular reviews of the service from our and our clients' perspectives. Only once did someone complain, and the evidence indicated they were just not in a good mood at the time they made their call; the receptionist had responded well and highly professionally to the situation.

We ended up engaging many other services from Greymouse, including emergency 24-hour technical assistance, graphics, research, and staff for call centre and administration. They provided a pool of resources to tap into as we needed and we only had to pay for what we used. Administratively this was also easy; with the outsourced company being Australian based all invoices were Australian so there were no exchange rate issues to deal with either.

Maybe I was lucky in the firm I chose. Not only was their business concept good but also the owners and I had a shared Mincom history, so a high trust level was already there. In my experience, outsourcing really is a super way to "beef up" resources in an affordable way.

For a while I was torn between my personal passions and the hard facts of business economics. The fact is it's not easy running a business in Australia, not only with the high salaries but abiding by all the industrial relations regulations, taxation and overall compliance requirements. There I was proudly publicly pronouncing that it was important to encourage women in technology and to grow technology businesses in Australia, yet in my business I had started to outsource to offshore resources. At least I was actively engaging females, but I was outsourcing many skills. This bothered me for a while, then I realised it was just a fact and I either did it or the business didn't survive. It wasn't a case of jobs here or jobs there, but jobs at all. So I got over it and over myself and continued outsourcing.

Some companies display their "corporate social responsibility" by building houses in poor countries. Perhaps giving them steady jobs is a better form of foreign aid.

I couldn't afford Australian rates of pay for software engineers and all the associated conditions. After the initial development offshore, then bringing it back onshore, as our needs grew so did the requirement to increase the number of coders. It just wasn't possible within Australia. At that stage even one coder's salary was close to our entire revenue stream. So I went back to outsourcing.

It worked well enough for a few years, until the company we were using increased their rates till they were to almost equivalent to Australian ones. As a result, I shopped around and found another outsourced firm that had more economical rates, which meant we could have a team of four coders: one of our own who coordinated the efforts plus three from the outsourced firm. Again, that worked well enough.

The main lesson learnt was that it is very important to oversee this process. Otherwise, all you have are coders working on specific development tickets. Without a coordinator, you don't have any real design or architecture inputs, nor anyone who has the full picture of the system in their head (yes, in their head: real techies dream code and systems, sometimes dreaming being caught in a looping bug!). If you only have separate coders you don't have anyone who lives, breathes and knows and loves the product from a technical sensibility. It is imperative to have someone who holds an overall vision of what it is and where it is going. With this arrangement in place we underwent a complete refresh of the product. I became actively involved, doing the design concept and closely monitoring development, performing both project director and project management roles.

That new front end and code refresh turned out to be very timely. In the world of technology, products leapfrog over each other periodically, and it is important to stay fresh looking and up to date. The product refresh gave us an opportunity to remarket and renew excitement. And it came at an affordable price at the right time.

Angels and Grants

Start-up or a going concern? Going concern or start-up? In my experience there are a lot of assistance programs for start-ups in their first few years, and when you start publicly making a good turnover, interest levels from external parties mysteriously rise up again. However in the middle there is a gaping hole. One where you can feel both in the dark and lost.

After a few years of still not making a profit but slowly growing, or at least surviving economic downturns, I started to explore options to secure more funding for the company. I hit the trail to present to potential investors. This meant I presented to a series of small panels. I carefully prepared targeted slide decks, and tuned them after each presentations based on feedback. Although I discovered that feedback from different groups can contradict each other.

I used my recognised talent for delivering compelling presenting, yet we still had no takers. I received lots of positive feedback about my presentations and everyone wished me luck and other generic motherhood statements, but no offers of investment. Well, with the exception of one person who said, "I like your product. It's boring compliance and boring has possibilities." He subsequently joined us for a time as an advisor with a view towards future investment.

Two notable things happened with that advisor. The first thing he said at our initial board meeting was that we needed to change our product name. That did not go down well and was *not* the issue. The second was that he was keen to undertake sales cold calling, something we had never done in our sector. I was hesitant, as I knew that aged care facilities were always busy with scheduled activities that restricted access to people, for a lot of available time. But he was an advisor whom we had met through a respected investment channel, and we were looking for new ways to grow our company, so despite my hesitation I took his advice. Off I went with him to nearby aged care facilities.

What a disaster that turned out to be!

The first few places we visited we never got past the receptionist gate keeper, leaving our cards and brochures behind. None of these facilities contacted us, and I suspect our materials probably hit the bin rather than being delivered to the management team.

Then we arrived at a facility where on arrival the receptionist looked at us weirdly as I explained we were there to discuss governance, compliance and accreditation. She directed us to take a seat, where I sat daring to hope that maybe this cold call stuff could work. The management representative came to meet us, looking both anxious and nervous. He queried the reason for our visit, and as we explained who we were he became furious and kicked us off the premises. His fury was because when we mentioned accreditation, he and the receptionist had thought we were from the official Government accreditation agency on a spot check visit. When they found out we were there to market our product they exploded, with us disgraced and kicked out as a result.

What we did not know at the time was that a few days earlier, that specific facility had had a spot visit and did not fare well, so they were edgy before our disastrously suspicious visit. It's ironic that although they'd just had a bad experience with regulators and were nervous and afraid of more, their response to a product which could have helped them was not relief but enraged rejection. As *Monty Python* once said, "There's no pleasing some people."

In any case, I can say that was the worst reaction from a prospective client I have ever had. It certainly ended our relationship with that advisor and naturally no investment was forthcoming. I expect he was a tad embarrassed himself at the violence of the result of his "let's sell by cold calling" tactic.

Back to square one, both stirred and a bit shaken. With a dire need for a vodka martini.

Government grants and concessions came in mighty handy. We tapped into and both really needed and valued the Federal Government Research & Development Tax Concession. Our claims started small but as product development increased, they increased. Then after a few years they tapered off. One year I recall getting an $85,000 concession applied, which sounds great until you realise it meant we had spent at least $250,000 on research and development that year alone.

Another government activity that was worthwhile tapping into was local and state government supported trips to trade shows. We did this to explore the New Zealand marketplace, and had some success opening up that market. Being part of a government sponsored delegation tends to let small companies have wider exposure and the perception of professionalism, plus we often were invited to participate in organised media events as well. In the early days it's great for learning and understanding more about your markets of choice, while in mid-stream it's good for gathering leads and catching up with clients. Sometimes the only problem was the associated paperwork to secure the grant. In my experience I found that often local or state funded grants had a stricter governance overlay and took more time, paperwork and follow-up reports than Federal Government grants ten or more times the size. It is almost a bit like, mmm, $10,000 or $100,000, which one will I go for?

Naivety

Sometimes you, well I, can be too open and honest, and that is naïve in the often cutthroat world of business. After a number of years using a near shore facility, the main coder assigned to us at the company there had grown attached to us and us to her. However, she was not so enamoured with the outsourcing firm and was looking at departing. Without the near shore company knowing, I was secretly paying her extra as a motivation to remain with them. After a while though, she still wanted to leave. At her suggestion we looked at her working directly for us. It would cost me less and she would receive significantly more money. Good all round – except for the near shore facility losing our contract.

We could have just acted and done it. We were not inducing her to leave, indeed we had been paying her to stay with them, and she could have resigned and I could have picked her up. But I decided that in fairness I ought to let the near shore company know, so I arranged for a meeting where I explained up front what we were doing. I genuinely thought they would appreciate the heads up.

Semi-embarrassing to say, but boy was I stupidly naïve. Especially when part of the coder's motivation for leaving was how little of our large fees actually went to her. They reacted by engaging a lawyer and seeking to sue me for a significant amount of money, both for daring to pay her extra funds and for "poaching" her. What had I gotten myself into by opening my mouth?

By that stage I had our own lawyer, so I asked her to review the claims. Her simple and effective response was to ask me if I knew anyone at the company. I said not really, but that I did know the owner and CEO and we used to have a good relationship. He was the father of the nanny I had hired when I was in Jakarta when Thomas nearly died. My lawyer almost laughed and said have you spoken to him? I hadn't. So, based on her sage advice I did, we reconnected, had a good friendly chat and reached a far more acceptable arrangement.

It still cost me money to "take" the coder, but nothing like the cost, effort and damaged reputation of a lawsuit. The lesson is one I am really only learning now as I write this. Innocence and volunteering information does not really belong in business. You do need to be armed with a tough skin and to realise that others may not react the way you would. Or is the real lesson… it's not what you know, it's who you know?

After not learning that lesson I fell into a similar situation years later. However, this time there was a surprisingly positive outcome. We had engaged resources in Fiji, which made sense as it gave us phone coverage for our call centre from the early hours and was more affordable than in Australia. We were lucky to be offered the services of high achieving, talented Monika, who we all grew to love and admire. After a number of years Monika wanted to work directly with us. Guess what I did?

Yes, I arranged to talk directly with the company. I knew the owner and had worked with them before (story sounds familiar?), so we met. I talked about the situation and told her that Monika wanted to work directly with us, and we wanted her to do so. Then I stopped talking, dreading what was coming.

But this time, rather than setting a lawyer onto me, the owner, Marisa Wiman, smiled and said, "Why wouldn't I agree to that? I'm all about alleviating poverty and with Monika working directly with you, she will have achieved that goal." WOW, what a response, what a person! Someone who truly acts on what she says rather than just spouting words. A person of integrity. She actually lived and enacted her company mission.

Entitled Money

Some money ended up being unnecessarily wasted on extras for people, not because I volunteered it but because they demanded it.

At one time a person I had a good relationship with, as we had worked together previously, joined my company for a short while. Let's call her X. To my utter surprise, on a trip to Cairns X demonstrated that she expected far more than what was provided. As a small company not yet making ends meet, travel conditions were economy for everything, including shared accommodation. We were travelling to Cairns to give a demonstration to a huge potential client in the education sector. We had already passed through a few stages of acceptance and the demonstration was the next critical part of their selection process.

We arrived the night before the demonstration and had reserved the evening for practicing our demonstration. X had come from the corporate world of large expense accounts and benefits – significantly different to the budget of small companies who have zero fat to spare. The car hired was a small economical car and one X was not pleased with. I also found it small but the car was only to get us from place to place, so we didn't need anything fancy. The hotel I booked offered WiFi, but it turned out they only had it in a centralised area, not in the rooms. This was before I had outsourced travel arrangements to Corporate Traveller. I had made the bookings myself, and had fallen for "false advertising" saying they had WiFi. Well they did, just not as most people would expect. A trap – lied to by marketing! The lack of in-room WiFi made things more difficult but not impossible, as we could use the common area to work in.

However, that inconvenience was deemed unacceptable by X. So we jumped in the car, losing the pre-paid hotel, and located another hotel that seemed okay from the outside. X checked the room and refused to stay there as well. By that stage I was concerned by all the time we were wasting and our need to practice for the huge VIP demo, so I decided to spend the extra money and booked into a resort style hotel. X ordered food and drinks, and drank much more than what I would consider suitable before such a VIP demo.

Her performance the next day was affected and it would have contributed to us not getting the deal. From memory that was the end of her engagement with us.

X however was nothing compared to Y. Y joined us years later and carried a sense of entitlement in almost every way. Unfortunately, I only became aware of this style after signing the contract. It ended up costing me a lot of money. The employment contract clearly stated travel and expense conditions, however Y would only fly business class, which I refused to fund. As CEO and owner, I didn't even travel business class myself. Their compromise was full-priced flexible fares for themselves so they could use flight points to upgrade. This still cost me more than I found acceptable, as the usual arrangement was for the travel agent (Corporate Traveller) to book the best priced fare on the day. With Y's compromise that always meant the most expensive fare, and I didn't feel it was fair or right to pass those costs onto the client even when the client was technically paying for travel.

Y would only hire larger sized vehicles, never mid-sized, they used valet parking at airports, refused to share accommodation and insisted on their own quarters. And the list goes on. I was too soft and inconsistent: even though I didn't agree with their demands, I put up with them as I valued their experience and had high hopes and expectations for future returns to the company. But we expended a lot of energy trying to meet their needs, and of course wasted money as well. I and other representatives still feel a little bruised from that experience. Everyone had to learn new ways of working with and communicating with Y. It was an added stress to our working environment. It was my mistake in hiring them in a rush in a moment of excitement.

Once upon a time as part of recruitment I used to have people look at our company philosophy statement and chat with me about what part of it jumped out at them and why. It was a very useful tactic, as it revealed a lot about the core of the person and their underlying philosophy. As I started engaging mostly people I or other staff members had previously worked with or knew personally, that tactic was dropped. Instead people were hired based on a trusted relationship.

None of us actually knew Y, but they had worked with a company we knew, so I didn't apply the philosophical tactic. Y seemed so promising – another person whose greatest skill we saw turned out to be getting themselves hired. Our outsourced HR was kept busy almost from day one of engaging Y, working through associated issues and disputes.

Another money waster for us was business cards, not a huge sum but a frequent one. So much so that they had become a standing joke between me and my husband, because it seemed almost every time I purchased business cards for someone, they departed soon afterwards. It's a tricky balance, because you and new starters are keen to have cards, but when you don't really know how things will work out it's a gamble. Especially when before the explosion of print services online, many places only produced cards in lots of a thousand. Besides, one of my people was such a fast tracker that her role title kept changing far faster than she could use even 250 cards.

Once, in what I thought was a good solution, I had business cards made with a generic email and phone number, and people just wrote in their own name and mobile. I thought it was a good idea as it instantly had branding and anyone could have one. Alas, they were not popular with staff members. In 2020 when I was clearing out office stock, I threw away thousands of business cards, a trail of changed logos, changed role titles and past representatives. It was not only an environmental paper waste it was clearly a money waster too. Looking through them was a trip down memory lane for me. Perhaps post Coronavirus the entire concept of business cards will shift to digital, thus eliminating this issue for future companies.

With our changing software look and feel, logo and colour scheme, we ended up with significant printed waste through all the brochures that we had bulk printed then became out of date. Boxes and boxes of them. Such an environmental waste in the end, though perhaps we can look at it as carbon sequestration. For a while we decided to provide all material on a CD, but alas most people seemed to prefer printed material. Additionally, there are different expectations, some people want lots of detail, others very high level only, and naturally some in-between. Therefore we ended up with three ranges of brochures to suit individual expectations and interest levels. Maybe post Coronavirus, with global escalating interests in improved environmental management and our increasingly online lives, the perceived desire and need for printed brochures will change.

Some money I just decided to let go of. While I was keen to win new clients, sometimes there was also a point where the 80:20 rule applied. Meaning, in this instance, if 20% of the clients are causing 80% of the pain then it is time to look at that and rethink. To me, as a small values-based company in the software business, clients were about building and maintaining a relationship that included mutual respect. If that respect was lost, then it was time to review the situation. On more than one occasion, when some clients fell into that 80:20 category, I spoke up and discussed the issues with those clients and considered where and how we could proceed.

Once in a brave move, I "sacked" a strategic client (read large and bringing in a good chunk of revenue) with whom staff had been having ongoing, serious issues with. The client was not demonstrating any respect and was behaving badly. I found it unacceptable and made the decision to remove them. They were shocked and promised improved behaviour. However having learnt my lesson from my first marriage, I doubted meaningful changes would ensue, so our agreement was terminated.

It wasn't a matter of clinging to clients for money's sake alone. Business is also about life and ought to include mutual respect. The positive effect internally from staff knowing that I had taken such a step to protect their wellbeing was worth gold.

***

Sonja's Tips: Money may only be a tool, but it does matter. Do watch and care where the money goes, and if as CEO you can't watch it closely enough, hire someone to do so.

12 To Be or Not to Be

Accidental Exit and Return

The greater part of our happiness or misery depends on our dispositions and not our circumstances –
Martha Washington

Sale! Wait, What Sale?

That was it.

I'd had enough. Enough of the company in-house personality dramas, enough of sale cycle disappointments. I'd just had enough.

It was a weekend at the end of August in 2017, when in a moment of weakness, I agreed to sell the company. The asking price was low (rock bottom actually), but I just wanted to get away. I didn't want to carry the burden anymore, didn't want to deal with interpersonal issues, didn't want to keep fighting the market. I just wanted out. I wanted to sell the baby and the bathwater!

My husband Robin was furious. He was in our home office at the time and couldn't help but hear my phone conversation with a sector colleague, agreeing to sell to his company. Robin questioned why I had done such a thing. My reaction… I got angry with him, saying it was my right to sell when I wanted, and that he didn't understand. I tried to explain the drain I was feeling, with two of my key staff members having ongoing personality disagreements and using me as the middle person in their interpersonal "wars", the disappointment over nearly getting there in multiple sales opportunities then not quite making it, the lost hope, the exhaustion. I outlined that the sale was to be swift and it all would be off my hands soon, and then I could focus on other things and be less stressed and over-wrought. I tried to put a good light on it. I explained that by combining the solution with this other company the end result would be significantly better for the sector. Selling my baby would give it wings. I tried to rationalise it to Robin and to myself.

After the agreement in principle and due diligence, the contracting process seemed to drag on and on, and that wasn't in my rationalisation. It was meant to be swift and off my hands. I wanted it done, finished, and for me to be out of there.

Sail Away

Then on 15 September, I went on a much-needed holiday. A cruise. Nineteen days of cruising on a heavenly itinerary: Hawaii, Papeete Tahiti, Moorea French Polynesia, Bora Bora, Wellington and Picton in New Zealand, then finally sailing into stunning Sydney Harbour at sunrise.

Before the cruise Robin, Kira and I holidayed in Hawaii. We flew into Hilo on the north east of the big island, and splashed out, renting a Mustang for the fun of the experience. We flew in a helicopter over live volcanos. This was before the Hawaiian volcanic eruptions in May 2018, and the pilot mentioned how one of the volcanos was overdue for an eruption. Maybe it listened. We landed at the foot of a giant drop waterfall and picnicked. It was magical and very, very relaxing. One night we visited the observatory at Mauna Kea and were amazed, listening in awe as the guide used his laser pointer to highlight key constellations. The drive up there took us through then above the cloud line and was fascinating. It filled me with inspiration and wonder.

As a child I used to lie on the roof of my cubby house looking at the clouds and imaging all the shapes and patterns. As an adult I know you fly above the clouds, but to actually drive above the clouds was an experience. That and misty mountains are things I particularly love in nature. Being there, experiencing that drive above the clouds and remembering my childhood joys began to restore my joy of life, and my internal strength.

Prior to the cruise, we transferred from Hilo to Waikiki and stayed at what today is still the best resort I have ever stayed at, The Kahala Hotel and Resort. It was stunning. Robin and Kira even got to swim and play with dolphins in the resort itself. I hope to go back there one day after Coronavirus travel restrictions and stay longer than just one night. Needless to say, this added up to a highly relaxing and "full of life's joys" atmosphere, where my mind and body began restoring themselves, and the weight of business stress started sliding away.

The day of the cruise arrived. School holidays were over, so we took Kira to the airport. She flew home to the Gold Coast into the care of my mother and back to school, while we continued onto the cruise itself.

For us it wasn't just a cruise. As a semi-retirement tactic, Robin and I had commenced cruise presentations. Since 2016, in our spare time (LOL) we've both given enrichment lecturers on cruise ships. This was also done in part to test whether the company could run without me, as sometimes itineraries meant I was away for a month at a time. I always delegated to a representative and ensured that business Will details were in place in case of a disaster.

We fell in love with cruise life from our first cruise in 2010 and decided to combine it with our love of knowledge and sharing that knowledge by becoming presenters. I speak on emerging technology and technology history, with subjects such as cryptocurrencies, blockchain and the history of the internet, and of course the history of women in technology; while Robin covers science from a philosophical view, with fascinating topics such as the ethics of Artificial Intelligence, time travel, and the morality of genetic engineering. We loved the work and from feedback knew that cruisers were surprised to have such interesting topics on board and had thoroughly enjoyed our talks. We've even had people thank us because they didn't want to cruise but their partner did, or whatever other reason, and attending our talks had made their cruise!

Sometimes it's a buzz feeling like a minor celebrity, as people ask to have photos taken with you, or stop you to tell you how much they loved "xyz".

This specific cruise we were on in September 2017 was Royal Caribbean's *Radiance of the Seas* and both of us had a full speaking schedule. Often it's just one of us as the speaker, or we share a single speaker slot with alternating talks. On this cruise, I had ten talks and Robin had eleven. It was a bit of work, but passion work we both loved and received a lot of satisfaction from. The speaking gig was only ever on days at sea, so we got to visit and enjoy all the ports.

All our talks went exceedingly well. I was overwhelmed at the level of interest in my Blockchain and Cryptocurrency talk. It was packed, with standing room only spilling out the doorway! There was even a Japanese fellow standing on the side near the front, showing so much interest that I interrupted my talk to walk over to him and ask if he was Satoshi. If you are not across Blockchain history the Satoshi reference will be lost on you, but I had already told the story to the room. Satoshi Nakomoto is the pseudonym of the mysterious creator of bitcoin using blockchain, who authored the original bitcoin White Paper. So all enjoyed the slight distraction. That talk was before the price of bitcoin went skyrocketing up the charts from US$5,000 to over US$20,000. Maybe some listeners bought then sold some bitcoin based on my tips of how to buy, and are now enjoying those benefits!

If so, you may contact me through my publisher.

First stop: Tahiti. I was eagerly awaiting Tahiti, as I grew up with memories of the Imperial Leather advertisement, the one in the private jet where the woman in the spa bath says, "Tahiti looks nice…" Sadly for me Tahiti, well Papeete, was not as nice as I'd been expecting. It looked as if it was decaying. In fact, in places it was literally decaying, on the hillside was an abandoned former luxury hotel. Just rotting away, not reused for a hospital or school or homeless accommodation, just rotting where it stood, as a sad, sad reminder of past glory days. I didn't know it at the time but have since found out that there are numerous such abandoned hotels and resorts around the world.

In 2018, when on another cruise, we found one outside Ponta Delgada in the Azores, Portugal, that was abandoned even before completion. It had a stunning view over the blue and green lakes (Lagoa das Sete Cidades), but must have been abandoned for a reason. Somewhere in there I think my mind drew a parallel of a once thriving business being left to rot, and a small niggle began about "giving away" my business being akin to abandoning it to rot.

The next port was Moorea, also in French Polynesia only ten nautical miles from Tahiti. Moorea was lovely, and we indulged in the shark and stingray feeding experience and chilled out on a beach hideaway; I am not a pineapple person, but I have to say the pineapples they served were exceptional.

However, Bora Bora was the icing on the cake. It was stunning. We snorkelled, swam with turtles, sailed, were soothed by local ukulele playing and singing by our guide, who was an incredible specimen of a man. And he knew it, posing for photos flexing his muscles and smiling (and flirting). He was a charming and funny man. His name was pronounced "OhNo", and everyone on the boat had an exceptional time due to his style. Half the women wanted to marry him, and possibly half the men. I still have his photo on my fridge at home and used to have one Blu-tacked to my daily computer.

It was heaven. Well it was joyous life on earth actually.

Changing My Mind

By the time the cruise pulled into New Zealand my head was completely cleared, my body relaxed, my energy restored, and I felt reinvigorated to take on the business again. I knew that I would call the sale off. I was fully recharged.

I believe I may have been extremely exhausted when I agreed to the sale. Sadness from exhaustion is not a usual emotion for me. Disappointment is my strongest negative emotion, and the emotion I feel most is happiness. Luckily the cruise saved me and the company.

On my return, I let the buyer know the sale was off. He was gracious about it, which was good, so maybe the company was having second thoughts anyway. We had known each other through the industry for a handful of years, and in particular through our voluntary involvement with the Aged Care IT Vendors Association (ACIVA), where I had also served as the committee's treasurer for a year. These kinds of shared experiences tend to build a camaraderie and increased trust level, which may have contributed to him being gracious when I advised him of my final decision.

I returned to my business with my own internal batteries fully charged, ready to re-energise the company. Although the in-house battle of the two strong personalities continued, I was more able to cope. I sent them on courses for managing difficult people (the other person is always the difficult one who needs managing!), shared their personality types with each other so they gained a better understanding of each other's motivators, and I engaged an HR professional for each to check in with and discuss any issues. My accidental exit and return meant that instead of a few hundred thousand dollars, I retired a few years later with multiple millions, which I can now use to put into place business angel activity that I have dreamed of doing. Thank you cruise life and in particular Bora Bora. There is a photo of me leaning back on the sailboat, and in my life I have never seen myself looking so relaxed. The place worked magic for sure.

I took away a few valuable lessons from that "no sale" though. Importantly for the final sale of the company, I learnt to ensure that more documentation was in place for the future buyer, as otherwise it becomes a point for them to reduce the sale price. In particular, all contracts and agreements needed to be clear and readily available: for clients, staff and partners. We had some, but not all, at that stage and many were out of date. So after the no sale I chased up the rest for a complete record.

I also learnt, hopefully, to never make a decision when emotionally charged, at either end of the scale of emotions, but especially if feeling exhausted or sad. Wait and recover first. If, after making a key decision you feel you need to rationalise it to yourself, maybe that is a message in itself.

Midlife Crisis

One topic that is rarely raised, and almost never taken into business considerations, is menopause. It appears to be a major taboo topic.

And if you cringed as you read that, you identify with it being taboo.

Menopause is almost an accidental exit and return in itself.

While I was already through menopause when this potential acquisition presented itself, there may have been some residual impacts that affected me, especially on top of being already being rundown and exhausted. However, the impacts of menopause are never recognised or taken into consideration, or even spoken about.

In the early days when my company was contracted to run mentoring and women's coaching workshops, one of our guest presenters, a person in a director general role in the public service, did a specific talk on menopause. Most of the female audience were shocked to hear it so openly spoken about. Yet all agreed that the impacts on business were significant enough that it ought to be included along with the regular depression and mental health discussions. But at that time, and possibly still today, it was not.

It's a fact of life and no one can run away from it. Yet even mothers don't often discuss this part of every woman's life with their children. And you certainly do not see it as a topic of discussion at business conferences.

From 2000 to 2002 I had had a few suspected miscarriages, and one fairly dramatic one, while I was hosting a VIP table at a significant WIT event. My guests on that table included the Mayor of Brisbane, leading CEOs of major corporates and a politician. While merrily engaging in networking chatter with my VIP's I realised something was awry. Something was happening to my body. I excused myself went to the bathroom and realised I was beginning to miscarry. The angst I felt was intense as I felt an obligation to both WIT and to my guests.

I cleaned up as best I could, and returned to the table, somewhat distracted, but there, nevertheless. I had to excuse myself a few more times during the event. The minute the proceedings finished, I rushed away asking a colleague to give my farewells to the table. I frantically called my husband and headed immediately home to the Gold Coast where he had arranged a doctor's appointment for me that resulted in a chemical womb cleanse.

Then in 2002, at the age of 43, I had a blighted ovum pregnancy and a resulting medical procedure, with a recommendation from the hospital doctor that, due to my age, and my prior miscarriages, I go on the pill to prevent ongoing miscarriage issues. After discussing this with my husband, who really didn't want me to go on the pill, I was also convinced. We both still held hope that we could have a child of our own. So I didn't take the pill, and shortly afterwards, we headed off on holiday to lovely Vanuatu and the most glorious snorkelling in our lives. Almost immediately after that holiday I then headed over to Malaysia on a business trip.

While in Malaysia I realised that I had missed a period. At 43 I didn't know if that meant I was menopausal or pregnant. Off to the pharmacy I went and purchased two tests, one for menopause and the other for pregnancy. I was hedging my bets.

I did the pregnancy test first and it was positive, but both my husband and I were sceptical of the results and the viability. On arrival back home in Australia I took another pregnancy test that was also positive. And in May

2003, at the age of 44 I delivered a delightful healthy baby girl, Kira Charlotte.

Just In Time, because within a handful of years I did become menopausal.

I had a long menopause, lasting approximately ten years. I tried all the natural treatments, but none worked, so I started Hormone Replacement Therapy (HRT). I asked my mum about her experience; she fell into the "lucky" statistics of a short menopause, mostly symptom free. In fact, she said she only realised she was menopausal when she was at the shops and realised she hadn't bought any sanitary products for a long while so she must have stopped bleeding. For me it occurred at a time of important business growth and high stress, so symptoms on top of that made a sometimes explosive mix, which pre-HRT was difficult to control.

I recall those embarrassing moments in meetings when my internal temperature rose, and I felt my face and chest flush and knew it was visible, those conversations where my temper flared faster than I was even aware of. When I heard myself forcefully say things I didn't intend to say nor really mean.

I went on and off HRT, testing to see if it was still required. Once I thought I was clear, but alas had to restart. I think my poor husband bore the worst of it. It made me wonder if maybe, just maybe, menopause contributed to the statistics of marriages that suddenly break apart after being together for years. For us it was different, we married later in life, and luckily we were both strong and remained in love despite the storm clouds of menopause.

From a business point of view, that cloud can impact relationships, decisions, articulation and the ability to think clearly. It's not as if you can stop and halt all work due to menopause. I'm not even sure what solution is workable, apart from being aware of the difficulties menopause brings and understanding the impacts. I don't want it used as an excuse, but it is real and does impact people and their environments, so it needs some attention and care with less taboo surrounding it. Everyone has bad moods sometimes, so the issues are not unique to women, but long term hormonally driven mood swings do make life and work more difficult, and that foggy confused mind from hormonally triggered lack of sleep can wreak havoc with thinking.

It is good to be on either side of menopause, but when going through menopause it is like exiting your regular life and work and going into a new land, to then return from it and be recharged again.

Pre The No Sale

The company was never styled to be a Unicorn – a start-up tech company with investor funds that reaches a valuation of at least a billion dollars – named after the mythical creature to represent the statistical rarity of such a beast. Instead, we were a founders' company, funded from owners' resources, which some have termed a Zebra – still exotic but more real and far more common. I also had no real exit plan. I had dreams, but no strategically thought out and crafted, targeted plan. Yet circumstances had bubbled around me, and as the hairs on my head became greyer, the thought of retiring began to rise in importance.

I only had limited experience of the potential business exit sale cycle before the accidental sale and return. Those few sales experiences had resulted in dead ends. Once, when a large corporate was in the early stages of looking at us, I was full of hope, thinking that the positive conversations assured that an offer would be made. I wasn't across the multiple stages of an exit. However, it did not proceed even to full due diligence, it just stopped. Part of my optimism was because I knew they were interested in entering the aged care and community care markets. Additionally, I knew and was known to all bar one of the board members of that company, and being already known helps with credibility.

The interest had been initiated by me anyway. One weekend I decided to reach out and test if there was any potential interest, so I contacted the founder, who responded swiftly and then contacted the Chief Operating Officer to talk to us. I had mistakenly thought that this swift interest would carry over to a sale. In the end, I think it never even made it to the board. We were very small then, with sales below half a million per annum, so perhaps we failed their preliminary criteria.

I did fail to learn from that experience, approaching subsequent offers of interest with open innocence and opening the company books far too early in the discussions. I now think that some mystery needs to be kept for later, so potential buyers become interested in the potential first. Mysteries such as full book disclosure and detailed code review should wait until signing on for due diligence.

After the No Sale

After returning from the cruise in 2017 I put my energy back into the company. It was a time of significant sector reforms and increased awareness, so my renewed energy paid off. I also refreshed the company with new branding, logos and more professional marketing materials. While testing different types of trade shows for their value for our platform, at one small business exhibition our lead marketing representative came across a values-based marketing company she introduced to me. Culturally they were a great fit. They were small and cared for their staff and clients. So I decided to explore marketing promotional options with them, and this led to an "accidental" rebranding and renewed awareness raising.

In a great example of how work and family life can mix even during business acceleration, in 2018 my son, Tom, was selected as Runner 39 in the Commonwealth Games Queen's Baton Relay. I flew Mum, Naomi, Kira and myself off to Adelaide in readiness for his leg of the run. As we arrived at our hotel, I received a vital work phone call. It was a major organisation and the last negotiation talk pre them agreeing to become a customer of my business.

I let them know I was in transit but delighted to take the call. I used hand gestures to explain to my family that I needed to take the call, sat in the foyer of the hotel and dived into the negotiations. Agreement was reached and my company had gained a new large strategic client. I got up, smiling, and returned to the family, checking into the hotel and refocusing on the pride of my son in the relay.

However whatever I did to build the business, ultimately I think it was external factors out of my control that made the major impact on the eventual sale. In October 2018, the Royal Commission into Aged Care commenced. The lead up to that resulted in increased market interest, which turned into sales with a reduced sales cycle. Prior to that, sales cycles sometimes extended to five years. With swifter decision making from potential clients, the company grew more rapidly. It's a sad fact that fear can be a strong sales motivator compared to strategic thinking about better processes and future benefits. In this instance, the fear of the commission and of the possible consequences of not having systems in place triggered a significant uptake in the market.

In 2019 I was attending a round table with other female technology business owners, when a lead member of the Department of Foreign Affairs and Trade asked the classic question that's been asked for decades: "What can the Government do to assist small business grow?" Well, I knew I ought to say, "reduce the tax burden," but instead I jokingly (well, half-jokingly) said, "Call a Royal Commission into every sector!"

I then went on to explain how the threat of a Royal Commission, then an actual commission into aged care, meant my business had grown at least 300%. Joking aside though, I do believe that governments should only take such actions for other, valid reasons, not just to benefit companies who provide products which protect the targets.

The growth continued. Even more so when the focus of the Commission became Governance and Risk. With our solution being Governance, Risk Management and Compliance with a focus on Quality, it seemed the ideal circumstance for drawing industry attention to the benefits of our product and the importance of having proper systems in place.

The increased sector focus once the Royal Commission was announced, meant that "the vultures came out", even before it actually commenced. Well not exactly, but it meant that many saw the opportunity it presented, and a handful of firms approached me to discuss potential investment, partnership and/or acquisition. For them to approach us in the first place, we obviously had to be a recognised name. That's the readiness part that can be undertaken in preparation for a potential sale. Ensure that your company name is on trade show lists, that the CEO or other representatives comment on media (traditional or social), and your web site is up to date with suitable content and search words.

My company had a casual, open knowledge and discussion style – transparency was central to our operations. Despite that I needed to be cautious to not disclose that we were looking at options for selling the business. When it was time to demonstrate the product to interested firms, I used a trusted representative whom I knew would not leak information to clients or other staff. If anyone wondered why we were demonstrating outside our client space, we could simply note that we were looking at potential business partners.

By then I was armed with more knowledge and experience of the process. Plus perhaps a touch of cynicism. We went down the pathway with one interesting company in a health-aligned space, that was seeking to add aged care governance and risk to its portfolio, and which seemed to have a fair and synergistic approach. Though initially it looked promising, after more detailed discussions neither Robin nor I thought the terms of that deal were favourable given the rapid growth rate of the sector. So, after a series of meetings and emails, that sale process halted.

In 2019, two investor-type firms approached us. They had different styles. One was a traditional investment, where they would buy in and we would continue to work for a set time in what was basically the same company but with different ownership. The other was interested in strategic future value through combined, synergistic platforms. We didn't pursue the traditional one much, as by then we were aware it was a formula valuation whose main benefit was a cash injection, without additional benefits for growing the company. The other offer was of more potential interest, as it was about strategic sector alignment. They weren't in a major rush so we both took it slowly, waiting to see how each quarter's results increased, prior to discussions on valuation and acquisition.

Interestingly, both the health space and one of the investor firms had approached us through recommendations from people I knew in the sector. We didn't chase anyone. As our finances had improved into a far healthier state, I was considering approaching a mergers and acquisitions firm to be listed, but it never got to that stage. I knew one of the partners of the M&A firm I had in mind; we shared a Mincom history and I had considered that if I listed the company I'd do it through her firm. But I didn't want to do so until we were consistently in a seven-figure financial stage. Thanks to the Royal Commission we were definitely at that stage now. However, time ran away from me, and then the final interested party swooped in and the deal was done.

***

Sonja's Tips: Both internal and external environments can make a drastic influence on what you do and how the business performs. The external you may not be able to control, the internal may be beyond your insight to identify and control.

Girls Do IT Too

Circa 2001- Damian sharing a Turkish lunch (an official ThoughtWare company meetup).

Girls Do IT Too

The Big Tick

'Virtual' office life gives balance

Women all over the world are turning their backs on corporate business, seeking the flexibility that the Small Office Home Office (SOHO) promises. Queensland Women looks at a Gold Coast IT company where strategic planning meetings include rattles, bottles and spreadsheets.

ThoughtWare Australia Pty Ltd provides software and services primarily to the information and communications technology (ICT), biotechnology and scientific sectors.

It has 11 core staff and a turnover of around $650,000, fitting the typical profile of IT businesses in Australia.

But its philosophy to work sets ThoughtWare apart.

"It is dynamic, it is fast-paced, it can be stressful, so to balance that, it is important to have a philosophy that both accepts the realities of the industry and values the individual," explained ThoughtWare CFO Sonja Bernhardt.

"Bearing that in mind, and building on my own experiences, we've created a work environment that is flexible so that balance in life can be achieved and the risk of burnout minimised.

"As a single parent working for 15 years in the corporate world, I experienced the full gamut of child-related issues - child care, illness, school events, guilt, stress, and desire for flexible work hours.

"I've made sure these issues have been minimised in a way that has encouraged active work participation and balance with home life.

"It works well for us. Our practices mean zero absenteeism. We retain staff because we look after one another; we have respect.

"It makes business sense recruiting and training new staff is expensive and staff have accumulated knowledge that is hard to replace."

ThoughtWare project manager Simone Files is one worker who has experienced first-hand the reality of the family-friendly policies.

"Three and a half years of working for ThoughtWare has seen me work full-time, part-time and casually from home and on client sites, take two lots of paid maternity leave for the birth of my sons Harrison and Jack (15 months the first time, followed by five months), relocate three times within Brisbane and now a final move to Toowoomba to be closer to family," said Simone.

"My level of pay has been adjusted on numerous occasions to take into account what I am working on, and how much I need to receive to survive on a reduced income.

22 | Queensland Women

Leading the way with Remote Office Working way back in 2004.

"We've worked it out together and ThoughtWare has always supported me, understanding the importance of family and balancing this with the business requirements."

Her experience is echoed by co-worker Janet Savage. "As a mother of three young children, my family's needs take first priority. Work requirements for me need to be flexible. The projects I have undertaken for ThoughtWare include data entry and research work, a style of work that enables me to work from home and at my convenience for long or short periods of time. This flexibility allows time for 'stress free' thorough completion of projects."

ThoughtWare staff work together in a 'virtual' sense using technology and a knowledge management system to hook up their home-based offices, gathering at Sonja's base on the Gold Coast for regular updates and planning sessions - complete with children, rattles, bottles, nappies, coffee, laptops and spreadsheets.

Sonja sees such progressive practices as the way of the future, particularly for IT firms wanting to attract and retain female staff.

"There's an increasing need within the IT sector to be good communicators, to understand business needs and the client, rather than just be technical - and that's good news for women who tend to be naturally communicative," said Sonja.

ThoughtWare Australia was a finalist in the National Work and Family Awards in both the First Steps and Small Business categories in 2001.

Strategic planning family-friendly style at ThoughtWare Australia.

SEPTEMBER 2004 | 23

Remote Office Work page 2.

SIMONE FILES - THOUGHTWARE AUSTRALIA

Vision finally becomes reality

Simone Files spends her day managing a team of people, disbursed across south-east Queensland and overseas, on behalf of a Gold Coast technology company.

And she does it all from her home office in Toowoomba.

Flexible hours and technology such as Skype and MSN Messenger make it possible.

Simone believes if you find something that you love to do, you will never work a day in your life. And she's living the truth of it by determining her own schedule to balance family life with her other commitments.

"Deciding what days and hours I spend in my office fits in perfectly with raising our two boys," said Simone.

Simone has been instrumental in developing software to assist small and medium sized businesses to supervise, analyse, and optimise their staff.

Two years into the project, her vision is now a reality with ThoughtWare ready to launch its i.on my software nationwide.

Childcare centres, private schools and professional practices are some of those businesses who will benefit.

The software is industry specific and not a generalised human resource system giving business owners and managers more time to do what they do best.

"The industries that we have developed the i.on my system for have a large percentage of their operating costs as staff costs," said Simone.

"Maximising staff productivity, by easing the administrative and compliance burden, results in huge savings in costs and time."

For more information on the i.on my product range, contact Simone Files on 1300 659 506 or email simonef@ionmy.com.au.

ThoughtWare Australia
Phone 1300 659 506
Email: simonef@ionmy.com.au • Web: www.ionmy.com.au

Media Promotion Credit The Toowoomba Chronicle.

Shayne Kake
Multimedia Developer,
ThoughtWare Australia

"Our BIT@Work student has contributed in a multitude of different ways that has resulted in an immediate enhancement of our perceived professionalism. From day one, he was creating marketing material, as well as enhancing our tender response templates and tools, then he moved onto software product front end improvements and an overhaul of our website."

Images from the University Poster promoting the joint degree and work program. Credit- Griffith University Shayne.

Natasha Hurst
Business Analyst,
ThoughtWare Australia

"We provide critical software to the aged care industry and in our instance our BIT@Work student arrived with the right skill mix and very importantly an excellent attitude to work and motivation to learn and continuously improve. I am already wondering how we survived without her."

Natasha.

Robin and I ready for a New Years Eve Roman Philosophy salon at our home.

2010- David Cooke NEC handshake locking in the cloud computing agreement with NEC and IonMy.

The remote conference in 2009. A lot of effort went into building a remote delivery platform we even included early stage Artificial Intelligence bots for questions and answers. Ahead of the times....

2009 Remote Conference Hall.

The 2013 face to face ion conference.

ion Conference2013 Gala Event group photo.

Free software will help fill out the paperwork

Jason Clout

A trio of IT businesses has combined to offer a rare deal: downloading their products free for a year.

The companies – B-free, Legal Toolbox and ThoughtWare – have provided a no-cost software option for 1000 small businesses entitled the Small Business Stimulus Package.

Chief executive of ThoughtWare, Sonja Bernhardt, said it was a decision taken to help other small businesses deal with compliance, risk management and preparing their business activity statements.

"They can just take the software they like, they don't have to take all of it," she said.

"Any business in Australia can access it. However, we don't want overseas users as it's for local businesses."

"It's really for micro, small and medium-sized businesses, like ourselves. Other than that it's just the first 1000 to apply."

Ms Bernhardt said if there was any "catch" to the deal, it was simply that at the end of the 12-month period, the users would like the product so much they would decide to renew their access for an annual fee of about $150.

"We hope they can see enough benefit in the products to renew. We stress that the offer is only for a 12-month period.

"But if they don't renew, their data is returned to them at our cost and in a useable format. There is an element of extending brand awareness for us through this project. But it's more that the way forward for small businesses is not government handouts, but to improve their productivity, which will also leave them better prepared for when the economy turns around," she said.

ThoughtWare's software contribution, i.on.my.business, had recorded strong growth in the March quarter. Sales were up 77 per cent on the same quarter in 2008 and the business's profitability had also improved.

"We're not multimillionaires, but we're doing OK and that's why we've decided to make this offer," Ms Bernhardt said. "As it's software, we can do it without it costing too much, although there are costs involved such as the extra traffic on our servers."

Many small businesses struggle with financial reporting. Ms Bernhardt said B-free's product expedited preparation of a firm's BAS, allowing the owners to concentrate on running the business.

The global financial crisis had left many small businesses vulnerable, she said.

"But if we can help them with their compliance and legal affairs, that might assist them through this difficult period. We'd like to see other businesses make a similar offer – small business helping other small businesses."

Newspaper promotion for the Target1000 campaign. (Courier Mail _ Gold Coast Bulletin_).

Staff photo at the Q1 face to face Conference. L to R; Simon (NZ), Tasha, Angela, Tiffany, Sonja, Kim, Robin, Kelly, Kay, Mardi.

Bali Retreat Workshop Back L to R- Amelia, Tasha, Sonja, Samara, Monika Front L to R- Selly, Michelle.

Surfers Paradise Retreat Workshop Dinner L to R around the table- Tiffany, Cheryl, Mark, Monika, Michelle, Veronica, Alison.

Bali workshop at work The workshop included great social activities, a visit to the bali office and zooming in others for some sessions.

Working at the Surfers Paradise retreat. Had to use the windows as the view was amazing.

2009- Natasha with early stage marketing care (aged), schools, centre (kids) and practice logos and when we provided CD's instead of paper brochures.

Then we focused on the purple care branding – where we sometimes mixed in red_orange Kim, Tasha and that back is mine.

2007- We started with the generic business logo with an orange theme.

Then focusing back on the care sector we returned to purple but with new logo and overall branding. This is certainly more subtle than prior branding. And is the branding that brought our attention to the buyer L to R- Monika, Michelle, Alex.

Right- Followed by bold blue and red. We did stand out! L to R- Tasha, Tiffany, Lydia, Michele, Sonja, Robin.

Girls Do IT Too

2019- Software engineers working hard. Amelia, Selly and back view of Tasha.

In readiness for a client and prospects cocktail event we held in late 2015. Sonja, Tasha, Kim.

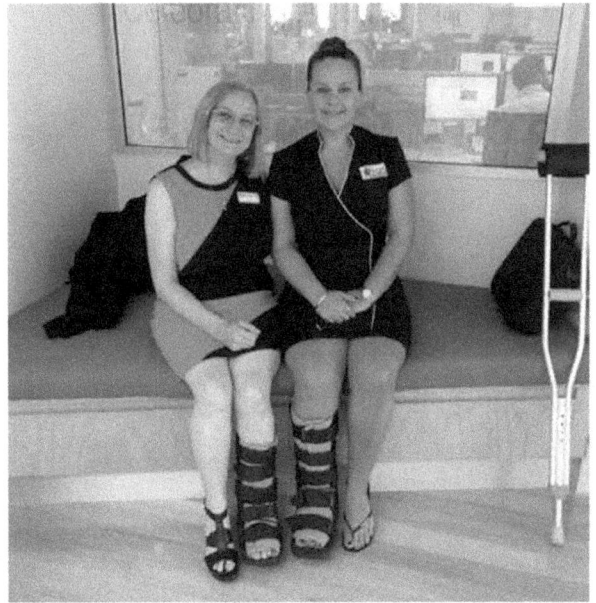

Early 2016- Work hard, play hard. Both Tiffany and myself broke an ankle at different events, but it was hilarious to find each other at the fracture clinic, and to then later attend product demonstrations together.

2015- Michelle and Tiffany in the home office.

Girls Do IT Too

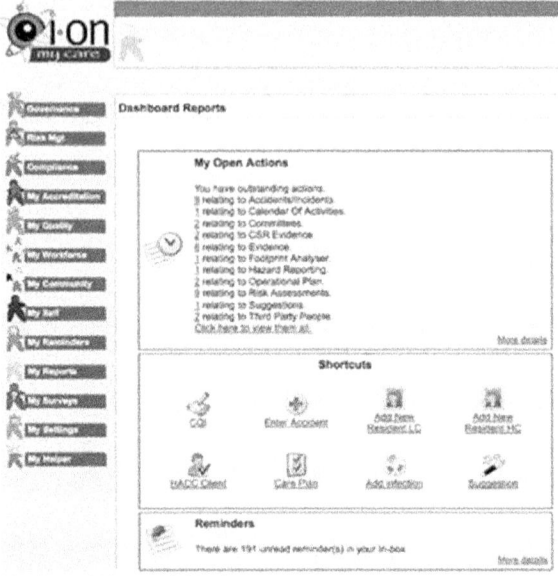

Internally we called this one 'Jelly Babies'.

This was our version 3 Upgrade look.

Version 4 'windows_tiles' look.

After being awarded the OAM, in my home office surrounded by our changing logo, posters and software. The board on the far left has pictures of Hedy Lamarr, Ada Lovelace and Grace Hopper.

2017- Hawaii Kira and Robin swimming with Dolphins inside the hotel.

2017- Bora Bora "OhNo" ukulele playing while we paddled in the gorgeous clear sea. Yes that's me in the water, and no I wasn't checking out what it looks like!

Girls Do IT Too

2017- Bora Bora this picture of me says it all! I had relaxed and recovered and was ready to take back on the world.

2018 Commonwealth Games Queens Baton Relay. L to R Mum, Tom, Naomi, Kira.

Girls Do IT Too

The Sale and End of an Era

Girls Do IT Too

13 The Twilight Zone

The Exit Light Shines

When one door of happiness closes, another opens; but often we look so long at the closed door that we do not see the one which has opened for us – Helen Keller

---

The light at the end of the tunnel started shining in late 2019, but I was blind and did not see or react to it.

No, it wasn't my death light calling, yet in some ways the experience was like a mini death for me. And I don't mean the French *petite mort*.

Readiness

Over time the company had been through a few colour schemes and rebrandings, but with lights shining in our eyes and a lick of hope we undertook rebranding again in 2018. The new branding and colour scheme was great, and we and our clients loved it. It allowed us to have highly professional marketing materials developed and re-ignited our profile with a variety of social media campaigns. It also gave us an internal company refresh as well – we all fell totally back in love with our company and our product. We'd been in operation for a while, and we had a really effective team, but you can sometimes lose those connections to your core fundamentals. The rebranding refreshed all of us as well. Maybe it's like refreshing your life by buying a new set of clothes.

Luckily the rebranding was successful and well received, because when I first met with El Blaney from Foundry Productions, the company that did the rebranding, I specifically said, "El, let's get one thing straight: I'm not going to do a rebrand!" Yet somehow, we did. I guess that proves marketing can work. And it had that superb result. Plus, secretly I believe it contributed to the potential buyer finding us.

In late 2019 Michelle, our client success manager, was called by a potential buyer, not as a result of a conference or event, but as a cold call. None of us were aware of the buyer's company, nor had any knowledge of their key people. They were truly out of the blue. It is not unusual for all sorts of leads and contacts to be made at trade shows, but it was unusual to receive a direct call. Based on our experience, after further exploration most unsolicited leads ended up as dead ends.

In the early days I used to get so mega excited about all the contacts we'd make attending trade shows. I used to proudly count the volume of "leads" obtained and feel they were a measure of the success of the show. Only to then discover that some were not as they appeared, and others were the in-between people, such as lawyers, marketers, researchers and advertisers. I learnt to work through the list to sift out the few genuine potential clients.

More often than not we have made better returns from tradeshows where we had only a few quality pre-qualified leads, versus heaps and heaps of contact cards. I quickly learnt that the typical "trick" of having a "drop your business card here to win xyz" promotion only produced extra work for yourself, following up each card looking for the actual potential leads among the many who weren't interested at all and only wanted to be in the draw.

It's far better to only gather the contact details of those you have had a rich talk with. Ideally come prepared with a prequalification checklist and pose those questions to prospects you talk with, to help focus both you and them. We knew that, but rarely applied it, and instead mostly chatted generally to people without overlaying a structured process. I should have taken my own advice, and then perhaps we would have grown sooner.

At other times we paid higher level sponsorships at trade shows and conferences to be a special listed partner, which included the benefit of getting the attendee list. We only did this if they included actual contact details. Some shows and conferences offered it, but only with the name and organisation, which was fairly useless. My pet peeve is that most lists are provided with a mixed listing, meaning delegates are mixed in with trade stand holders, speakers and organisers. Many times, those others outnumber the real delegates, the potential clients, so a mixed list inflates the true numbers. For example, 500 people might be there, but in fact 280 of them are trade show representatives, 50 are speakers and 20 are organisers, leaving only 150 actual delegates. And of those delegates, there are often multiple representatives from the one organisation, so the real genuine possibilities are even lower.

Despite, or because of, those lessons, our process was to ensure no contacts were instantly eliminated but all were captured and ultimately contacted based on a prioritised list. In this instance two things happened. First, I was in December slow down mode, preparing for a Christmas and New Year cruise with lots of my family: my mum, all my brothers and sisters, my children and grandchildren, and many of my siblings' children. We were all off on Ovation of the Seas to New Zealand and return, a trip that had been two years in the planning. The second was I had wrongly assumed that as I hadn't heard of the prospect they would prove to be time wasters. So I wasn't really interested and didn't bother to rush to make contact. I was not convinced of any compelling reason to do so.

Reality

My family had a superb cruise. We hadn't all caught up together for many years and the ship was perfect for some all-together events, and smaller sub family activities and privacy if desired. Then on 30 January 2020 I received an email from the same prospective buyer. As January and February are traditionally slower months, and my colleague Michelle had followed me up to see if I had contacted them, I decided I would action it then.

I called and was shocked to realise that they sounded entirely professional and that their intention seemed genuine. However, based on past experiences I didn't trust my own judgement (some think I am prone to over-enthusiasm!), so I arranged for my husband, Robin, to come to Sydney with me to meet and explore the possibility further on 4 February. At that stage I still thought the visit would eliminate the lead. But again, it seemed to be genuine interest.

The company appeared to have done their research and certainly had a well-prepared and impressive plan laid out. They had a well-developed, strategic, whole of aged care sector strategy planned, and had already pulled together highly impressive people, other products to be part of that plan, and powerful marketing material such as videos and brochures. It was clear that they did know and understand the sector well, had the "right" connections, knew the sector pain points, and their approach was one that the sector desperately required.

I was convinced even from this early stage that they had the know-how and resources to pull it off and that the sector would gain immense value from their strategy. That visit was swiftly followed by some early stage due diligence. At this point we thought it was about potential partnering, where the interested party would take on board marketing for us, with our software being part of an overall platform of products they would sell. As such, after signing a confidentiality agreement between us, I agreed that some of our other representatives could pop in and out of their Sydney office, freely sharing our knowledge and knowhow, with our Sydney based staff member there on a daily basis.

On reflection I think they had engaged in a smart tactic of getting to know us, our people and solution through this approach. As things hotted up, Robin and I then revisited them on 19–20 February 2020. At the end of the first day, it became clear that their interest was in an acquisition, not a partnership or as a marketing agent. We walked back to our hotel in a bit of a shock, imagining what that may mean to us and the future. So began an evening of some serious discussions between Robin and I, where we agreed on our approach if offered a sale, and very importantly, our bottom-line price.

In a way it was a bad time to consider selling. After our years of hard slog, many factors were now pushing the industry toward our product, and the level of interest from larger clients was growing rapidly, along with our sales. Usually, buyers look to past performance for comfort. But we could see that if things continued the way they were going, the value to us of simple product sales could quickly outstrip the purchase price based on past or even current sales. We had already gone off one such sale for that reason. We had to consider what price would be high enough to make us comfortable giving up that potential future income, and that would be our bottom line.

I think knowing your bottom line, and the value you put on your business is important. Although in the end, as the generic saying goes, the value is in the eyes of the buyer, still it's a comfort and a starting point for negotiations for you to have some idea. A peg in the sand, so to say.

Then the pivotal day came: 20 February 2020. Just before the explosion of Coronavirus in Australia, we merrily waltzed back into their Sydney office, delighted the office was still there. Discussions had been going so well that we had been making jokes that maybe it would be like the offices in the Michael Douglas movie "The Game", and we'd find that what was a hub of activity previously would be an empty shell today. It all seemed a little surreal.

It wasn't. It was genuinely real.

After morning greetings and an introduction to the group executive, who had flown down overnight to join us, we were whisked into the office of the lead executive and an offer was put on the table. What a way to start a day! No coffee needed to jolt you awake when that happens.

Some solid reasoning ensued about the state of documentation, the business readiness, the security of the client base and the robustness of the technology. Luckily, based on lessons from our prior accidental exit and return, we had our client contracts and staff contracts all in place, and our discussion the night before ensured that we were armed with the data and evidence to defend our view. And so, with various concessions about timing and conditions, the offer increased to what was entirely acceptable to us. In fact it was in what for years had been my dream sale price range. Robin and I looked at each other, nodded, maybe smiled as well, then accepted. An agreement in principle was made.

I had agreed to sell my baby.

Handshakes all around. A third executive was brought in and advised of the full agreement and price, and they also agreed. More congratulations and handshakes.

Into the Twilight Zone

So why did it still feel surreal? Why was it still like something out of a book or movie? This was an entrepreneur's dream, and the offering price was my dream sale price. Where was my elation? Even champagne and congratulations didn't fix how I felt. I remember how I used to coach people when managing technology implementations projects, and how much everyone looked forward to "Go Live". Yet in reality when the go live date arrived it was almost always an anti-climax. The hard work and build up was valued of course, but the actual day often felt flat and surreal. To me I felt I was experiencing the same twilight zone syndrome.

They were in a rush to move and wanted to take over from Monday 24 February – only two business days away. It was being done on goodwill, faith and trust as contracting was to follow, but we were confident the terms of the deal would be sorted. In fact, as we sat in the Virgin Lounge for our return flight back to the Gold Coast Robin drafted the Term Sheet. We'd elected to craft it so that all of our understanding was included. They, of course, were mega busy in readiness for taking on board new clients, new software and new staff, so it made sense for us to do up the term sheet.

We did this with our internal knowledge that until the contract signing was complete, we were always able to "take back" the operations. Some controls were still in place so we could restore full control back to ourselves if something went wrong. For example the buyer was introduced to clients only as new management due to increased growth. Emails and contact details remained the same, all front end staff remained the same, full access to key IP remained with us, and the news was not released to media.

In my heart I had become closely aligned to the aged care sector we operated in and like many others "wanted to make a difference". To me the buyer's strategic whole of sector plan would make that difference. I knew that as a single small operator my difference so far had been, well, single and small, whereas an entire sector plan with impressive players and serious backing could make a more significant difference. Mentally and emotionally I had signed onto their future plan, and that was a big contributor towards agreeing to the sale. I would not be abandoning my baby, I would be handing it over to a good family who could do things I had not been able to achieve on my own.

What a rush, in one way! Except it still felt unreal to me. I was wandering around in a daze the way you do when you get bad news and suddenly you seem insulated and isolated; things continue to go on around you, but you feel odd and weird, trapped in a surreal world. Disassociated.

Anyway, Monday 24 February rolled around and a "mandatory" all-staff meeting was held – remotely of course, as our people were geographically scattered. In a move that many during Coronavirus lockdown might relate to, there was a technical glitch getting the remote meeting started at the buyer's end. The delayed start didn't go down well as people were on the edge of their seats as to why this meeting had been called and wanted to know what was going on. There had never been a mystery mandatory meeting for everyone called before.

In my anxiety, I fiddled with my computer screen, you know adjusting it to get a more attractive view of myself and the room – except I accidentally pulled out the power plug, so in a panic and state of high anxiety I had to rush to restart my computer and relog in.

The meeting started 15 minutes late when the buyers zoomed in, literally via Zoom. I spent some time letting everyone know the software business was now in the hands of the new owners, effective immediately. I went through a lot of the reasoning for the "handover", such as them being a larger company with more resources and better positioned to manage the growth. Then I handed over to the new owners and I left the meeting.

Perhaps my accidentally pulling out the power plug was symbolic, as if I had pulled the plug on the business. And I had, in some way.

The news wasn't a big shock for the two staff representatives who had been closely involved with the buyer already. However, it was for the remainder. But I think there isn't really any other way to do this sort of thing. Regardless of internal company transparency and communication, I feel that decisions of this magnitude need to be done by stealth without everyone being involved until "official" announcement time. After all, it's human nature is to worry and feel your job is at risk, and as we had learned with potential acquisitions before, usually these processes end up as nothing. So why frighten staff unnecessarily with an unknown? Besides, in this instance the decision to sell came as a shock even to ourselves, the business owners.

At that time, our web site listed us as a company of twenty-two people, made up of two business owners supported by legal, accounting, marketing, travel, HR and general advisors plus fourteen staff spanning Queensland (six), Tasmania, Victoria and New South Wales (one in each), plus three in Indonesia and two in Fiji. As those staff were either employees or contractors for whom we had grown to be a major part of their work and income, almost instantly the usual rumblings of job insecurity started, with people wondering what would happen to themselves and their jobs.

In the Zoom meeting the new owner had said that it would be business as usual. Actually, he used the acronym "BAU", which provided an amusing illustration of the difference between us and our larger buyer. Not being a "corporate" firm, I had not generally used corporate-speak in conversation in the company before, so a number of our people didn't even know what BAU was, and later asked me what it meant.

Naturally, at times of change and possibly more so with unexpected change, people's concerns for their future rise. I spent some time privately reassuring people that work would continue and indeed would grow under the new owners. Additionally, I advised our other outsourced functions such as our legal and travel people of the business change.

Somewhere in there I cried.

In a move that I rationalise as a way to make the transition faster, the new owner almost cut me off. From day one they took over, and I was on the outer. I had expected to remain semi-involved or at least to be consulted for a few months. However, the cut was almost instantaneous. I felt hollow and adrift with nothing to do.

Of course, when one sells their company, one ought to expect they are no longer involved. I did think that I might be needed for some time, but cold turkey it was. Without a doubt my being around would have had an influence on the staff, with them leaning on me or old ways of doing things, and likely this would have delayed implementing the changes. Over time I had learnt that me just being there sitting at a table had an influence, without even opening my mouth. Rather than me being considered of no value, I now think of this like what I used to say to project managers: "Those managers whose projects fall apart when they go on a break are poor project managers, while those who can go away and things run smoothly without them have done a superb job, because it means processes are in place and the machine is well oiled."

Not needing me must have meant I had done a good job – right?

I remember years before I was managing a project for a major emergency services department and the project sponsor never felt comfortable if things seemed under control. She only believed a project was a real project if there was something visible causing issues that needed sorting. She pointed to other projects where when the managers went away the project suffered issues, yet with mine I was barely required: trying to imply I wasn't needed, or that I didn't know the project enough to identify the pain issues. Even then I knew the issue wasn't my project management style. I did change though. I started escalating minor issues, making sure that the project sponsor heard of them to help address her need to have drama around a project. Sometimes project management requires "managing" not only the people under you, but the people over you.

After the Sale

What happened to me after making the decision to sell my baby?

The first few months were hard, very hard. Adjusting from being busy with stretches of very busy to doing almost nothing was no easy feat. Despite it being because I'd achieved a dream goal, it was still difficult. My mind and body were used to decades of a "habit" of being busy, and to suddenly be out of that habit and anchorless was a shock to my system.

Some "normality" was in there the week after the handover, as we were already booked to attend a sector conference/trade show. I was a speaker at that event, so even though the new owners manned the stand with the trade stand team, I was still in attendance. It was so weird for me, being there but not assisting at the stand, and not saying anything to clients as they greeted me or sector colleagues as we spoke. It was again rather Twilight Zone, with me a ghost haunting my previous life.

One incident at the conference should have given me a clue to both my own issues in letting go and the nature of an operating officer working for the new owner. She pulled me aside for a chat, but that chat rapidly ended up with flared tempers where she was very disrespectful to me, instead of seeking guidance and advice. I walked away saying, "I don't have to sell to you at all." She arranged for the lead executive to call me and try to calm things down, but in hindsight the nature of my reaction to her different communication style was a telling sign.

Another "normal" activity was we had a speaking cruise lined up in March which we'd booked long before the sale, proving that we practice what we preach about being able to go away without our companies collapsing without us. This was a cruise where both Robin and I spoke, sharing a full-time speaker spot on the stunningly lovely Cunard *Queen Elizabeth*. We had never cruised with Cunard before, and both of us fell in love with the ship and its classic elegant style. Plus, they treat their speakers very, very well.

We sailed out of Sydney on 9 March 2020. The original itinerary was to sail to Singapore, but now that Coronavirus was making itself known the schedule was adjusted to a series of Australian ports then off to New Zealand, for nineteen days in total. The ship was stunning and the entertainment fabulous.

We did our first talks and both were well received. Mine was on blockchain, and I had included three Australian women[xii] and their companies. A male audience member congratulated me on profiling Australian female business owners. I quipped "Thanks for mentioning that, Google me and you'll see it's what I do, I'm known for supporting and promoting women in technology."

In another talk I was to give on cryptocurrencies I had two other Australian women to flag[xiii]. Unfortunately, though, I never got to present more than once, as due to increased Coronavirus activity New Zealand closed its border to Australia, so naturally the cruise was cut short to seven days, disembarking back into Sydney.

In a reflection of our own experience managing the sale of our company, the discussions and decisions had been made some time before passengers and crew were advised. We remember seeing small knots of staff whispering in little nooks later, no doubt stressing over what would happen to them.

While it was disappointing for our speaking cruise to be cut short, I was also relieved, as we had our teenage daughter back at home being cared for by my mum. With the uncertainty of the virus I wanted to be at home with them, so the cruise finishing on 15 March worked well. It was scary enough when the ship pulled into Port Arthur in Tasmania and all the cruise staff were wearing surgical masks. The world soon got used to people masking up, but at that time it was the first bulk mask occasion I had witnessed, and it scared me a little.

The ill-fated, Coronavirus-ridden *Ruby Princess* docked only four days later on 19 March. No one on *Queen Elizabeth* had reported unwell, and self-isolation wasn't in place then, so at least we avoided an extended quarantine. Subsequent reports did not identify anyone on Cunard's QE ship as infected.

Even before self-isolation became a thing, we sort of did it. Instead of our daughter Kira catching the train to school (she went to school in Brisbane and spent almost three hours travelling back and forth on trains each day), on my return from the cruise I drove her to and from school. When I wasn't driving I mostly stayed at home, as did my husband. After one week of driving back and forth, back and forth every day, and the virus taking a stronger hold all around the globe and with my husband in an at-risk category, I thought it was best if our daughter remained at home, so I requested remote learning for her. What I was not aware of was that was just about to be introduced for the next school term, so it was readily agreed to.

That early stage Coronavirus anxiety distracted me a little from the post-sale blues, or perhaps it simply delayed the blues.

Another activity that helped distract from or delay the blues was that we had just completed a house extension and it was ready to move into, so I spent a number of weeks setting up and settling into the extension. The hilarity of that project was that almost half of the extension was designed as a larger home office, which, ummm, was no longer required so much given the sale. Oops.

One habit I was having extreme difficulty with was emails and the compulsive urge to check them. I was used to checking emails at the start of every day and prioritising things to do as a result, as well as continuing to check during the day as further work-related emails arrived. The cold turkey approach meant I went straight from hundreds of emails a day to a handful. This meant I went from at least an hour of checking emails at the start of the day down to a few minutes, even seconds. Yet my mind and body still insisted on those early morning checks and all-day monitoring of both emails and skype messages, which had dropped to zero. I felt like something was missing. It was almost like losing someone or something.

That's probably not a bad analogy. It felt a bit like mourning.

We had intended the deal to be signed before our cruise, however it turned out to be more complex than we thought. As a result we were still ironing out the contract details and the tax implications, which was a major learning point. If not done carefully, the Tax Office considers that the entire sale value is taxable in the year the sale is made. Because the buyer was paying in tranches over several years, and indeed paying nothing significant at all for over a year, if the entire tax bill was due at the start it would simply be impossible to proceed.

We would go broke from the tax bill, let alone be able to take advantage of the success of an exit. It could have meant we owed millions in tax immediately, years before we had the funds to pay it. Or in cases like ours where the final figures are dependent on future growth, you can even end up paying more in tax than you eventually receive. Crazy I know, but it is what it is and a trap those seeking to sell their baby need to be across before agreeing to sell. It is safest to assume that the tax office thinks of it all as "their" money unless proven otherwise. I had no idea and we had already agreed to sell. We'd mostly handed over the day to day operations, so it was a little complex and stressful.

Luckily my youngest sister, Sarah, is a taxation lawyer and brilliant at it. She gave us early advice, and also connected us to the right professionals to nut it through in terms of the contract. But because of the complexity and the time needed to structure things properly, our original theory that full contract signing would proceed mere days after agreement in principle proved false. Instead, we were left with having effectively handed over control of the business with no proper contract and no payment, on nothing but a Term Sheet, trust in the buyer, and our belief that we could still claw it all back if we had to.

Robin and I experienced some extreme stress related to finalising the contract, the tax and adjusting to the different way the buyer communicated. In truth, and this will sound odd given that I agreed to sell on faith, in some ways I ended up not trusting or believing the buyer. We still sometimes wondered whether if we went back there, we would find their office an empty shell. I certainly became critical of their new way of doing things. They appeared less efficient than we had ever been and they certainly demonstrated far slower turnaround times, and in part I resented them not seeking my advice or input on certain aspects. I figure that was part of me not fully letting go.

On the plus side they were already proving to be commercially more successful than I had been, securing sales with large organisations that had been out of my reach, yet some part of me just didn't like it. I struggled with why and how an organisation I saw as less efficient than us could be almost instantly more successful in the market. Again, my issue in failing to let go.

We continued in a contractual twilight zone for months. This was made worse by everything being slowed down by the Coronavirus lockdowns. Eventually we had to set a deadline for the signing of the contract: before midnight on 30 June 2020. All the in good faith pre-activity and then stressful contract negotiations after the handover meant we were well and truly ready for that date. The final pieces fell into place and literally a few minutes before midnight the formal contract was signed. Just in time.

That was it: The deal was done. It was official, I had sold my baby.

***

Sonja's Tips: The buyer finds you. You can chase potential buyers, but I think ultimately, they find you. The value is in the eyes of the buyer, but you can assist in adding to that value by being ready: be armed with your evidence and ensure your "ducks are in a row". And understand the tax implications of the way a deal is structured.

14 To Retirement and Beyond

It's a Whole New World

One never notices what has been done; some can only see what remains to be done – Marie Curie

---

It's a Numbers Game

Statistically, to be a female owner of a software development business with a financially successful exit places me in a unique category of the population. To be a business owner whose technology company consistently comprised at least 85% females, and where for most of its life all software engineers were female, again puts me in a statistically significant and interesting category.

In many ways, I feel that doing what I was passionate about was the best shining example of practising what I preached. To not only talk about women in technology being important, but to strike out, set up my own company and staff it with women in technology sent a very strong message. I hope…

At the time of the sale I was almost 61 years old. In my heart I have always been just a girl somewhere between the ages of 18 and 27. Now I need to take that inner perception and make (maybe take) the future to be mine.

There *is* a whole new world out there.

With the increasing probability of life extension, I may be around to catch the first wave and live a few hundred years or more but feel and look like I am 18 to 27 again. Luckily the healthy sale price of my software development business means I'm privileged enough to be able to do something meaningful going forward. I cannot yet fix the biological ageing and health issues I have, but I can continue to participate in something meaningful.

The Present

Being female, I will probably always live with the feeling of guilt of letting down my staff members. At the time of writing this memoir, five of my original team are no longer with the new owners. Four of them had been let go by them, one within two weeks of the hand over, two a few months later and another nine months after the sale. Another one resigned eight months into the handover. I was also aware that most of my ex-staff struggled with adjusting to the different way of operating, such as the loss of work hours flexibility. I carry some of that pain and all of my own self-induced guilt. But it was my decision to sell, and despite my guilt over the staff and their futures it was ultimately my business, and my responsibility to operate in a way that achieved my own happiness.

I guess one of the downsides of being a small, flexible company is that selling to a larger one often does mean a seismic shift for the staff into more traditional roles and processes. I have also subsequentially heard that it is not uncommon for those who sell their business to begin to feel critical of the new owners. To experience what I have.

After selling my baby, it took me approximately six months to settle and start to adjust to the change. I needed to accept that my own life was forever going to be different too. Part of the deal was that I was not allowed to be involved with, own, or even act as a consultant for a similar business for five years. I needed to accept that I no longer had any pressing need to frequently check emails, monitor and respond to Skype messages, catch up on a giant to-do list or make decisions affecting the business and its people. That's a whole lot of what used to give my life meaning just gone over night. I have always been one of those people who define themselves by themselves, and not by their work; yet still the habit of work forms strong bonds and is not an easy thing to break out of.

I have discovered that unsubscribing from the many lists I was on has helped me filter out messages that I used to seek and that informed me, but are now not useful to my new focus areas.

In many of my industry and school presentations I included the following advice: All you have to do in life is – focus on your life as your highest priority and your happiness as your responsibility. Combine that with get up one more time than you are knocked down, and your purpose and focus will happen.

And that's how I have lived my personal and work life. Now that I have achieved a major goal, it's not time to just stop. Focusing on my highest priority is still my responsibility.

I'm not one to sit back and do nothing.

At one stage my husband and I dreamed of owning a media empire just so that we could support books, movies, television shows and media stories that we felt were philosophically strong. We now have a generous amount of funding but not that much. I would have had to have sold for ten figures not eight to entertain that dream.

As part of my adjustment after the sale I figured that I needed to establish some kind of retirement schedule. To assist myself in establishing some kind of new routine, I drew up activities I'd like to begin to start. Coronavirus lockdown reminded me how much I loved nature, I discovered a new love of birds, and rediscovered my love of butterflies, so exploring those activities in my future feature high on my list. However, a large activity for me is to work out the best way to invest the funds. I have three children, three grandchildren and a lively mother that I would like to spoil a little as a result of my newfound wealth, hard-earned wealth, and of course there are ourselves – me, my husband and teenage daughter – to take care of. Plus, I have a deep desire to assist other female-owned technology firms, especially those in the middle stage of growth, that forgotten post-start-up, pre-visible success stage.

It may sound anal, but I created a spreadsheet on possible ways to invest the funds. I started one a number of years ago when I had stars in my eyes about a potential sale to a large corporation. After this sale I returned to that spreadsheet and tried out a variety of options. Top of the list is creating some type of fund for female owned technology companies. Which means I have a lot to learn about how such funds work and are created and managed. I have learnt that money vanishes much more readily than it grows.

Impulsive moments have featured heavily in my life but I want to ensure that with the female technology fund it is set up for sustainability. I'm not keen to add my money into another fund group, I want to leave my own legacy and I want some semi-active role. It will be good for my brain, and anything that can help stave off dementia is a great thing to undertake.

As my life story has demonstrated, new ideas, technologies and people have always excited me. The rapidly moving world of virtual reality, augmented reality, artificial intelligence, crypto currencies and blockchain is already making its impact felt in key areas such as health and education. The whole new world out there of those and other emerging technologies, shines with possibilities.

The Future of Women in Tech

I have led a life where I answered the call to address the lack of females in technology and it has played a significant part in my life. I have seen the issue wax and wane in the media and in the eyes of the public. I have been a pioneering warrior seeking to amplify the key message that life in IT was a great life worth pursuing.

After a lifetime of implementing and observing intervention activities, my strong and considered opinion based on my own active involvement and deep research is this: despite all the intervention activities in the world aiming to improve the female representation in technology fields, the most effective "getting on with it" approach is for women to set up their own technology firms and to actively engage other females in that company.

Maybe I am a tad biased there.

One way to nurture an environment to encourage female technology entrepreneurship may be to divert intervention funds into something more practical, for example as I noted in my first women in technology book: *If you add up the spending by all of the global projects, programs and research even just over the past five years, it is likely that the funds and efforts spent would have been enough to establish a major university focused solely on IT courses for women and a corporation to hire them.* That corporation to hire women in IT to give them a kick start *would* improve the numbers.

Do that or do nothing, and let the organically changing face of the world, society and the fascinating future technologies do their thing. Let it evolve into a world of individual empowerment and choice.

My Future

This book and life itself loudly send a message that – you just never know what's around the corner. Look at what 2020 brought us! That was not predicted, and I'm not going to predict my future either.

What I do know is that throughout my life I have always felt and demonstrated a great joy in life alongside consistency that is often made evident through my strong moral code and integrity.

I can say that I look forward to reaching out to my family and providing financial assistance, to the return of cruising, and also to establishing a fund for female owned technology firms that are beyond start up stage.

Oh and BRING ON reversing the effects of ageing as my young mind and spirit would seriously love the arthritis, osteoporosis and general ageing issues to go away.

***

Sonja's Tip: When I was social convenor at my university college and attending a formal event at another college, where I had an invite for two but snuck in myself and two other people, I drew some attention as apparently I looked like and spoke similarly to Marlene Dietrich. So instead of a quote from me to close this memoir I will quote *Marlene Dietrich*:

"There is a gigantic difference between earning a great deal of money and being rich."

I am lucky enough to have both.

Girls Do IT Too

2019 Robin and I in a company corporate pose.

2020 on board Ovation of the Seas Me and my children L to R- Naomi, me, Kira, Tom.

2020 on board Ovation of the Seas My smart, funny, lovely grandchildren with their parents Back L to R- Tom, Renee Front- Ava, Ella, Noah.

Epilogue

My Own Lessons

I love the quotes in my book and hope you did too. I selected each one and crafted my own to help amplify the key message of the specific chapter. These are key lessons in themselves. The main lesson threaded throughout my life is that the extra effort undertaken to get out and about to meet people and to build genuine respectful relationships with them provides not only warmth when writing one's memoirs, but also provides added value throughout both your business and personal life.

I also hope that between the stories and comments, the small lessons and tips for business, personal and common wisdom also made their way through. Below is my list of 61 of them. There are more, but I've selected just 61 because…well I was almost 61 at the time of the sale.

How did you go, how many did you glean?

Business (35)
- A deal is not a deal until the $ is in bank.
- Know what you are good at and not good at, and let others do the bits you are not good at. Or in other words master the art of delegation.
- Get your product out there in stealth mode and test it out before launching into mega marketing.
- Getting the pricing model right is *not* easy.
- The cemetery is full of irreplaceable people.
- Short courses and hands-on experience will keep tech skills up to date.
- Don't let yourself spend too much time on the "meet me for coffee" syndrome.
- Actions speak louder than labels, meaning what someone does and how they behave is a more accurate presentation of who they are than their role may imply.
- Respect and listen to the experts in their fields instead of assuming you know the solution.

- Sometimes good management just means getting out of the way.
- Entering awards frequently increases your probability of winning as you tune your responses each time.
- Sometimes winning an award may be due to unknown political or other criteria, so don't take a non-win personally.
- Sometimes things are not black and white and tough calls need to be made.
- Single mothers can make amazing project managers.
- Do not measure your success by others' perceptions.
- Even all the money in the world, high profile support and a great idea is no guarantee of success.
- Mates may be mates but do not assume because you know someone that less scrutiny and governance can be applied.
- Engage lawyers early, value their review of contracts and learn to ask if services provided are outsourced or sub-contracted.
- Ask your clients for input into product development.
- Bending rules, thinking you are being kind and helpful, may have the opposite effect to what you expect.
- Some people just do not like nor value working from home. People are individuals, some thrive in the extra responsibility and flexibility of working remotely, but some do not.
- Let go of CEO and founder ego and the feeling that only you can do it.
- Outsource all the functions you can, e.g., accounts, HR, travel and more.
- There is no one magic marketing bullet.
- You need to have on board all three skills: marketing, presales and sales closers. Preferably in three different people.
- Take the time to discover what individuals value as a reward, it's not always money.
- Give people a known incremental salary pathway rather than a big salary that doesn't change.
- The more you "give away" the more people expect that as the normal and the less they appreciate it.
- Set performance and benefits indicators for sponsorship activities, and measure against them.
- Financial governance is important, engage a CFO or appoint a financial person on your board.
- Nearshoring/outsourcing is a viable economical alternative.

- You can ready yourself for a potential future acquisition by ensuring your paperwork is in place.
- Mysteries such as full financial book disclosure and detailed code review should wait until signing on for due diligence.
- Rebranding does refresh. not only externally but internally as well.
- Managing means managing people over and under your position level.

Personal (17)
- When you get knocked down, get back up.
- Practice to build your persistence and resilience.
- Be true to yourself. Don't try to fit others' expectations.
- Get comfortable undergoing and accepting change.
- You never know who you will bump into from your past.
- The core of a person is who they are, not their physical appearance.
- Flexibility is king.
- People are just people regardless of their work role or social standing.
- Remain human, treat people as interesting people.
- Keep stretching yourself to continue earning and learning.
- Everything we experience contributes to who we are.
- Beware of rabbit holes, both personal and business.
- Learn to engage in hearty, open, honest and meaningful debate without taking offense.
- Take time out to consider what success means to you and follow that path.
- Try not to be an over-achiever.
- Do not be afraid to be brave.
- It is okay to immerse yourself in your sector, just don't lose yourself.

Common Wisdom (9)
- Build the relationship and the sale follows.
- Seek to understand others' expectations.
- Know what is in your control and what you can't control.
- Being in the right place at the right time does make a difference

- Learn to stop and focus on special moments.
- You have to start somewhere.
- So much of life requires careful planning, but so much can also depend on luck.
- Team sharing and celebrations are important.
- People really do only value what they pay for.

Girls Do IT Too

2010: Bletchley Park: Home of the Codebreakers. Me with Colossus Computer the world's first programmable electronic computer.

We were on holiday in England driving and I saw a sign to Bletchley Park and got excited telling my husband to detour and go there. At that stage he had no idea what it was. He, and I and young Kira ended up loving the visit. So historical and meaningful.

About the Author

Sonja Bernhardt OAM holds a BA, GDBA and an MBA. She retired in February 2020 after selling her software business.

Throughout her career Sonja has served on several technology related committees including United Nations bodies, APEC (Asia Pacific Economic Cooperation), Ministerial Advisory Boards, as well as prestigious national and state-based organisations. By so doing she has contributed significantly to the technology industry. This earned her a prestigious Medal of the Order of Australia (OAM) on Australia Day in 2011.

In addition, Sonja has two Technology Halls of Fame awards: in 2019 Sonja was elevated to the Pearcey Hall of Fame for her distinguished lifetime achievements and contribution to the development and growth of the Australian Information and Communications Technology Industry, and in 2005 she was inducted into the Women in Technology International Hall of Fame in Silicon Valley.

Sonja lives on the Gold Coast, Queensland, Australia with her husband Robin, daughter Kira and Papillon dog Oreo.

Discover more on: http://en.wikipedia.org/wiki/Sonja_Bernhardt and Sonja's personal blog site www.sonjabernhardt.com

Notes

[i] Available at https://www.igi-global.com/book/gender-inequality-potential-change-technology/211899
[ii] Available at https://www.igi-global.com/book/blockchain-technology-global-social-change/221876
[iii] Andrea, Aston, Chris and Debra, whom I engaged in the early years, then Michelle and Veronica in the company's later years.
[iv] Watch the shave here https://youtu.be/p7xS2fVxXdY
[v] Myself, Jenny Beresford, Anne McGill, Carolyn Hill, Bernadette Hyland, Liz Manning, Yvonne Packbier, Glenda Slingsby and Ann Uldridge; later joined by Sonya D'Aoust and Jeanette McLeod.
[vi] Dale Spender, Sheryle Moon (Accenture), Lynne Hackwood (Energex IT&T Manager) and Carolyn Baker (Australian Institute of Management). There were also two male presenters, both lecturers at QUT (Neville Myers and Wayne Bucklar).
[vii] Dave Redden from Oracle and David Usher from IBM
[viii] You may listen to the jingle at http://www.passionit.info (soundtrack to the video)
[ix] Available at https://www.igi-global.com/book/women-new-social-era/95023
[x] Jo Furey-Lopez, Amanda Markie and Peter Cranitch
[xi] ACAA (Aged Care Association Australia) and ACSA (Aged and Community Services Australia)
[xii] Leanne Kemp – Everledger, Katrina Donaghy – Civic Ledger and Jemma Green – Power Ledger.
[xiii] Jane Thomason and Loretta Joseph

www.ingramcontent.com/pod-product-compliance
Lightning Source LLC
Chambersburg PA
CBHW051536010526
44107CB00064B/2743